OLD WHITE MAN

CHRISTIAN
PATRIOT
DEPLORABLE?

Sam Powell

authorHOUSE®

AuthorHouse™
1663 Liberty Drive
Bloomington, IN 47403
www.authorhouse.com
Phone: 1 (800) 839-8640

Published by AuthorHouse 10/24/2019

ISBN: 978-1-7283-3207-9 (sc)
ISBN: 978-1-7283-3206-2 (e)

Print information available on the last page.

Dedication

I would like to dedicate it to:

Grace Church Thursday Morning Men's Bible Study.

CONTENTS

ACKNOWLEDGEMENT

I want to acknowledge Ken Faughn, a special friend with patience and time given me to get this book together. His ability to support my use of Microsoft Word has been a gift for which I will be forever grateful. I have been blessed with the many likes, loves, and comments of my many Facebook friends.

INTRODUCTION

I became a Facebook poster several years ago. As a technophobe, I have had a hard time learning how to apply all the bells, whistles, pictures, shares, and likes. I do know how to type, and put a sentence together, so as my number of friends grew, I began to write a post once a week. Trying to get attention, I dubbed it, "My Saturday evening post." Ever so often, someone would respond with, "You should write a book." Taking their advice after over a hundred posts, I've got a publisher. I've put together a small non-fiction, often with tongue in cheek, first book.

Today's tribal political culture has made it more difficult to practice the Golden Rule. I must always remind myself of God's love for everyone, even my enemies. I have been tabbed as an enemy of the progressive climate changers, and they have thrown me into the basket of deplorables. If you read this far, I hope you'll read some more. I believe our country is losing its way. Perhaps we have gotten too big for our britches. History has its own way of repeating itself, always seeking the truth, cursing the powerful, and blessing the weak. Change is always painful, yet pain is usually changeful. Change is fast for some, and not fast enough for others.

In these pages, I have written about politics, culture, history, sports, ups, downs, family, friends, heroes, and change. I have made light of things, and often worked hard to find the truth. It is always a special time for me when I settle on a topic and find out lots of things I never knew. My research is from books, movies, personal experience and the internet. The social scientists tell us we make 200-300 choices a day. If true, I've made over 5 million; lots of chances to make some bad ones. As I have aged my choice making skills have improved. I have learned the importance of acceptance, courage, and wisdom, and plan the continual pursuit of the truth. One truth, for sure in my lifetime, is the blessing of being a Texan.

If you were born and raised in Texas, you hit the big lottery jackpot. Texas is not only the greatest state in the world, but it's the best place to live, to work, to play, and to pray. Down here in Southern Flyover Country, the Heartland, the southmost area of our nation's breadbasket, we take pride in our people, our places, and all sorts of special things. Texas is also a state of mind. We're diverse, we're braggadocious, and we're friendly. We're also tough, kind, and neighborly. If you're not a Texan, you probably want to get here as soon as you can.

Most of my days, I have read the local newspaper. If I was impressed by something, or if I disagreed with an editorial opinion, I would fire off a letter to the editor of our stinking fish wrap. The editorial staff limited the words, thus I often struggled to get my point across. The current state of our written and spoken opinions have become so crass, one could just say either, "Your opinion is FUBAR," or, "As usual your opinion is SNAFU." By the way, those are not acronyms for some far-out gender definition.

I an old WASP. There, I've said it. And I'm male. The old, white, male, from Western Europe, usually a child of a mainline Protestant Christian family, is the endangered species of the 21st century. Most of my childhood friends were WASPs; so were our grandparents, and our mothers and fathers. In the big lottery of world humanity, we hit the jackpot. I think those old jackpots are rusty and getting shot full of holes.

If you were born in Texas, the American South, or the Midwest, you're my friend. Friendship is good, and as I grew up in Waco and Corpus Christi, Texas, everyone had lots of friends. As I got older, joined the Navy, officed inside the Beltway, spent six weeks training in One World Trade Center, I met many short-term friends. My current residence is in Northwest Corpus Christi, Texas, high above the banks of the Nueces River, and I have no plans to relocate in my old age.

Old white men never die, they just lose their privilege. Without privilege, we just keep on, keepin on, knowing the good Lord willing, the creek won't rise. Also, old Christian, Patriotic Veterans never die, but some of us become deplorable. Today, I wear my badge of Deplorability with honor. Recently, a Texas Patriotic Veteran told me in no uncertain terms, we were both racists. Simple me, replied, what makes you think that? His simple response was, "You're white aren't you." Alas, in my old age, I'm tasked with being a Racist, with no biases I might add.

So, read! My friends and you shall learn, a ride of joy, and days of fun. We've found some time to seek the truth and share ourselves with those we love. Each day gives new, each day dies old, moments go by, here comes another. Live each day with all you've got, yesterday is history, tomorrow is a mystery. HOOKEM!

BOOKS AND MOVIES

AUG 12, 2017,
THE VALUE OF ART

In 1987, Random House published another bestseller. "The Art of the Deal," was number one on the New York Times bestseller list for 13 weeks, and stayed on the list for 48 weeks. I had heard of Donald Trump, but this page turner introduced me to one of the great business negotiators of all time.

When Trump became the GOP candidate for President, I had to read it again. My favorite chapter was the account of rebuilding the Wollman Ice Rink in Central Park. What a story of government waste, and the courage and brass of a private citizen to make chicken salad out of chicken you know what.

The chapter begins with a timeline starting in 1980. The New York Parks Department closed the ice rink for renovations. It was reported it would take two and a half years to complete the project. Also, in 1980, construction began on the Trump Tower. It was completed in two and a half years. The Donald's apartment overlooked Central Park, and from his living room he could see the floundering fiasco of the Wollman Rink. By 1986, he couldn't take it anymore. Trump wrote, "I just got fed up one day and decided to do something about it." He called Mayor Koch, and made a fabulous offer to take over the construction.

After six years of starts and stops and after millions of dollars the City was back at square one. Trump made a generous offer to Mayor Koch, and built a new Wollman Ice Rink in six months, on time and under budget. I did a bit of research on the construction project. Trump's account was accurate.

This story reinforced my belief in the power of the private market, and the genius of the American entrepreneur. Almost all governments evolve to waste and corruption. And as these problems grow, the people's freedoms decline. I am reminded of Benjamin Franklin's words when he walked out of Independence Hall after the completion of the Constitution. He was asked, what did the founders give the people? He said, "A Republic, if you can keep it."

JUL 15, 2017,

HAVE WE BEEN BORKED?

How far are we from Gomorrah? In 1996, Robert Bork's book, "Slouching Towards Gomorrah," outlined an excellent wake up call for America. Unfortunately, his warning went for naught. One must believe his message of moral and cultural decline was gravely misunderstood. Gomorrah was a wicked city on the plains east of the Dead Sea. Ancient history tells us it was destroyed by God. Judge Bork was nominated to the Supreme Court by President Reagan. A warped Senate, plagued by secularism, hubris, and cynicism failed to confirm this brilliant jurist.

Are there any Gomorrah's today? I can think of a few possibilities, but the city winning, "Most Wicked," is surely the area contained by the Beltway surrounding the District of Columbia. It's so bad there, the ones who are able, live just outside the Beltway. Are there any real American statesmen in those many office buildings where most of government's elected and appointed officials ply their daily works of waste, fraud, and corruption?

Our new Wheeler Dealer, Commander in Chief, wants to drain the swamp, a noble goal, but will he find a place where these misfits can dry up? My mind drifts to Guantanamo.

It was refreshing to read the complaints of Jamie Dimon, the CEO of JP Morgan Chase, the largest bank in the USA. Yesterday, it was reported in the New York Post, Mr. Dimon went on an epic rant, ripping Washington bureaucrats for their chronic dysfunction, and inability to get anything done. He was quoted, "It's almost an embarrassment being an American citizen traveling around the world and listening to the stupid s - - t we have to deal with in this country." The quote continues with more appropriate criticism. Yes, we may very well be, "Slouching to Gomorrah."

Dimon's words are paradoxical, as the big Wall Street Bankers have more control over government than the total population of flyover country. As a deplorable I wonder where that Massachusetts Native American Senator, always speaking with forked tongue, would stand when considering Mr. Dimon's remarks.

Her tribespeople lean to the side of occupy Wall Street, but her campaign can't do without those rich donors from New York.

My, my, what funny thoughts...a great jurist, a bigtime banker, and an elected faux squaw, all concerned about our seat of government, located on the Potomac Bubble, over ten thousand miles from the plains, east of the Dead Sea.

APRIL 8, 2017

CODE OF THE WEST

Shortly after the end of the Civil War, in 1865, when our country was still torn apart, Horace Greeley, editor of the, "New York Tribune," wrote, "Washington is not a place to live in. The rents are high, the food is bad, the dust is disgusting, and the morals are deplorable. Go West, young man, go West and grow up with the country." After over 150 years, our nation's capital has not changed much. Perhaps, the food may be a bit better, but the dust is still disgusting.

Many did go West, and many wonderful accounts reflect the exciting history of the American Frontier. One of my favorites has been the Western Cowboy. He has been glorified with fascinating short stories, novels, movies, and beautiful art. About ten years I came across a splendid book, written by an investment banker, and illustrated by a superb, Western photographer. The author was James P. Owen, and photography was by David R. Stoecklein. The title is, "Cowboy Ethics: What Wall Street Can Learn from the Code of the West."

Owen lists ten tenets, just as appropriate today as they were for the Cowboys who rode for the great ranches of our American West. I challenge you to find the book and benefit from the truths found there. Anyone who has lived by these ethical standards has lived a life well done. Each of the ten are equally wise in their teaching, but one really got my attention: "Remember Some Things Are Not for Sale." These words have stood the test of time. They stand as a memorial to all the good things for which our country stands.

I believe many, if not most, of our national, state, and local leaders; elected and appointed, have forgotten the meaning of these words. All of us need to think about our own, "Things," which we would never sell. I pray our leaders would never sell their vote, never sell their commitment to us, never sell our country's honor, and for all of us, we should never sell our word.

This cowboy wouldn't sell his horse or his vote.

AUGUST 25, 2018

KINGDOM OF HEAVEN

NINE/ELEVEN! How soon we forget the darkest Tuesday of our lives. Americans packed the pews the following Sunday. Still fresh in our minds, we tried to fathom the airborne terror slamming into the two World Trade Centers, another hijacked plane crashing into the Pentagon, and a fourth going down in rural Pennsylvania after the bravery of its American passengers. Over three thousand innocent dead. Thousands injured.

How quickly Osama Bin Laden shouted to the world his hatred for the, "Great Satan." Headlines decried the evil of terrorism. Politicians rallied against the radical Islamic terrorists. Our President stood strong and patriotic, calling for all of us to stand together against this act of war. Many of us remembered our history all the way back to the Crusades.

Sadly, less than a year later, Easter of 2002, church attendance had dropped to pre 9/11 numbers. This reality is troubling. So much has happened in the Middle East over the past seventeen years, a suicide bombing in Afghanistan hardly makes the news. Why do I rehash this tragedy? It's because of a movie I missed back in 2005. I watched it on cable this week, and I had to watch it again. "Kingdom of Heaven," is an attention getting title. Great casting, Orlando Bloom, Liam Neeson, Edward Norton, and others played medieval characters involved in the Crusades of the 11th and 12th centuries.

"Kingdom of Heaven," is historical fiction, but its message is important. In massive detail, thousands of Christian warriors are pitted against more than thousands of Muslim warriors. It's a bloody fight for the city of Jerusalem. I won't give you the rest of the plot as I don't want to spoil it.

I do want us to remember our history. In the Middle Ages, the Muslims had conquered much of Christendom. With more and more encroachment into Europe, there began a call to free Christian brothers who had been enslaved and tortured at the hands of the Muslim Caliphate.

Pope Urban II, leader of the Catholic Church during the 11th century, has been quoted (with documentation), "How does a man love his neighbor as himself, when, knowing his Christian brothers in faith and in name are held by the perfidious Muslims in strict confinement and weighed down by the yoke of heaviest servitude? How does he not devote himself to the task of freeing them? Is it by choice you do not know many thousands of Christians are bound in slavery and imprisoned with innumerable torments?" As Popes go, Urban was a bit more wordy than most, but he got his point across. During the 11th and 12th centuries the Church regained its place, and freed thousands of Christians throughout the Middle East.

Is it telling that Columbus reached the Western

Hemisphere in 1492, the same year the Muslims were finally routed from Spain? Perhaps. What is surely telling is the continuous fighting in the Middle East. This crossroad of history is the birthplace of three great religions. Judaism, Christianity, and Islam. All three preach the, "Golden Rule. Love your neighbor as yourself." Will we ever learn?

MARCH 10, 2018

THREE BILLBOARDS

Did anyone watch the Oscars last Sunday night? Nope, me neither. However, I have a slight interest in the movies and actors winning the miniature C3PO's. My TV fare is limited to several channels amid hundreds of less than middling choices; however, I found a program on Monday naming the winners. Frances McDormand won best actress for, "Three Billboards to Ebbington, Missouri." Although I knew nothing about the movie, I took my bride to see it this week. Both of us enjoyed the flick, with some reservations. The female lead was easily recognized as she played the lead in the movie, "Fargo," about 20 years ago. She won best actress for Fargo as well.

Dark comedy identifies, "Three Billboards." I laughed out loud several times, embarrassed by my outbursts. Several of the scenes reached a rare combination of hilarity, combined with outrageous vulgarity, high anger, and extreme violence. While the dialogue was over the top—filthy, the acting was superb. If you can put up with the cussing, you may enjoy the show.

The film is fictional, and Ebbington, Missouri, does

not exist; however, small towns across our country are very much in existence. Many of these towns used to be the backbone of the USA, but now they are dying out as urban and suburban populations are thriving, at least as far as population growth is considered. Ebbington is an ugly portrayal of small town America, and I know the scene did not accurately reflect the hundreds of small towns that dot our nation's heartland.

Studying USA's history, Post World War II, has been a pastime of mine for the last ten years. There are both a wealth and a dearth of cultural, economic, political, and societal analyses attempting to understand both the growth and the decline of America. "Three Billboards," is successful in depicting the worst of our culture. The screenwriter, while talented, is rooted in anger toward society in general; my opinion based on his early years as a financial failure.

The movie took me back to two books I read five or six years ago. One, "The Unwinding, An Inner History of the New America," by George Packer. Two, "Coming Apart, The State of White America, 1960-2010," by Charles Murray. He qualifies his use of White America, by stating, "The trends I describe exist independently of ethnic heritage." Packer is from the intellectually elite, from California with intellectual elite parents, but also has roots in the deep South, where his grandfather represented the Alabama Ninth Congressional District, primarily the city of Birmingham. Murray is also an intellectual elite, one of a few from Newton, Iowa. He is a well-known political scientist, being a graduate of Harvard, with a PHD in Political Science from MIT. While Packer writes for himself and the New Yorker, Murray is a Senior Scholar with the American Enterprise Institute. Packer leans toward the Progressives, while Murray's politics are basically Libertarian. Both writers did a stint in the Peace Corps.

I bring these two excellent thinkers together as they both arrive at similar conclusions with thorough, but different methods of research. Both books were great reads, and I am in agreement with most of their findings. I quote from, Packer's prologue, "No one can say when the unwinding began---when the coil that held Americans together in its secure and sometimes stifling grip first gave way. Like any great change, the unwinding began at countless times, in countless ways---and at some moment the country, always the same country, crossed a line of history and became irretrievably different." Murray includes a statement in his prologue, "This book is about an evolution in American society that has taken place since November 21, 1963, leading to the formation of classes that are different in kind and in their degree of separation from anything the nation has ever known. I will argue the divergence into these separate classes, if it continues, will end what has made America, America."

I believe it is telling when great minds with different political persuasions come to agreement. Both thinkers are very learned and have done their homework when reaching opinions and conclusions. Each expresses a similar concern with the decline in community, culture, society, and economic opportunities.

My singular, original offering is to shout loudly across our once exceptional country, "WAKE UP AMERICA.!!!@#&*$%/---YOU DON'T WANT TO UNWIND OR COME APART LIKE THE PEOPLE FROM EBBINGTON, MO."

FEBRUARY 23, 2019

SOUTHERN LIVING VERSUS DEEP HATE

Fiction often tells us the truth! As an old white male, it is easy to understand the consistency of America's history. We can learn a great deal by reading novels describing the greatness of our country. The talented writers of every generation have enlightened us about the good and the bad. We can take comfort in our, "America the Beautiful," and its ability to shine through whatever ugliness gets in the way.

The history of the Deep South overflows with honor, dignity, beauty, reverence, and hospitality. There is also the underbelly of conflict, class, flawed character, and at times, man's inhumanity toward his neighbor. As a teenage student, I believed the passage of the 13th, 14th, and 15th Amendments righted the wrongs of inequality's evidence, which had clearly denied the freedoms granted in our founding documents.

How do you compare Mark Twain's, "Huckleberry Finn," with Harriet Beecher Stowe's, "Uncle Tom's Cabin?" Or, how about Harper Lee's, "To Kill a Mockingbird," and Louis L' Amour's, "The Sacketts?" There are truths in all of these American novels. The characters tell us truths about ourselves. There were times when I wanted to be like Huck Finn, and I didn't want to be like Simon Legree. My heroes have always been cowboys, and I knew I could never be such a man of character and kindness as Atticus Finch.

Recently I finished a new, great American novel of the Deep South. "Mississippi Blood," by Greg Iles was published in 2017. Writer Iles grew up in Natchez, Mississippi, and the book takes place in and around this southern town on the eastern bank of the Mississippi River.

In the book, is a fictional editorial written by a fictional, mixed blooded talented female journalist. I would like to share the two and a half page account, but I would lose you for sure. Here is a sample of the truths I found. "Because of the proliferation of mass media, the twentieth century seems filled with such cultural dividing lines: the assassinations of John F. Kennedy and Martin Luther King Jr.; Woodstock; Nixon's resignation; the L.A. riots; the O.J. verdict. They are different, but they share one trait: they unite millions of people by revealing some hidden truth about the nation." The truths are the tragedies, the violence, the justice and injustice, the need to escape and the need to find each other.

Mississippi Blood is a story about a white southern gentleman doctor, filled with earned respect, and a white evil clansman, filled with hate for the black man. There are many other well-developed characters with a wide spectrum of respect and hate. There's a sentence which capsules the book's title. "Mississippi blood is different. It's got some river in it. Delta soil, turpentine, asbestos, cotton, and poison. But there's strength in it, too. Strength that's been beat but not broke."

There are approximately 1,000 known hate groups in the U.S.A. They come in many different colors, different beliefs, and different tragic ideologies. They lost or never had the experience of caring, sharing, and loving. Their lives are a miserable lot. The crazy feeling I have as an old white man, is the truth of God's love for them, just as I know he loves me.

ITALIAN APPRECIATION FOR MUSIC

My text for today is from the, "Green Book," an excellent film up for five Oscars, and based on a most unlikely, true story. It's a must see! If you search for, "Green Book," make sure you add, "Movie." When Blacks traveled by auto, mainly in the Deep South from the 1930's to the 1960's they relied on the, "Green Book for the Negro Motorist." Now collectors' items, the books were helpful to know which hotels and restaurants would provide service to Blacks during these last decades of the, "Jim Crow," era. I feel uneducated since I didn't learn of the book's existence, until I saw the recent hit movie, starring Viggo Mortenson, up for best actor, and Mahershala Ali, nominated for best supporting actor. It is also up for best original screenplay and best picture.

As an aside, If you just google, "Green Book," you might get mixed up with the wrong Green Book, or the short title for, "Standards for Internal Control in the Federal Government," published by the U.S. Government Accountability Office. This so called, "Green Book," couldn't help you get from the White House to the Capitol

Building. Just the introduction includes, Five Components, Seventeen Principles, and numerous Principle Attributes; all of these to assist government employees and contractors to be more efficient. OMG!

The authentic Green Book proved to be a helpful travel guide for Blacks, as they traveled in the Deep South, from the 1930's until the last was published in 1967. I'm sure Martin Luther King would have been pleased the '67 edition was the last.

Now, to the movie. I hope you see it; a superb account of two men, very different, but very special. Mahershala Ali plays the part of Don Shirley, a Black child prodigy, of Jamaican roots, with the ability to play the piano on a par with Arthur Rubenstein. Due to segregation, and unable to play with the best symphonies, he created popular classical, jazz pieces, and became well known throughout the country as the leader of the Don Shirley Trio. The Trio included Shirley on the piano, and included a bassist, and a cellist. I would have preferred a percussionist instead of a cellist, but perhaps due to Shirley's piano virtuosity, a jazz trap set wouldn't have worked.

In the early '60's Shirley had himself booked throughout the Deep South for a concert tour, and needed a driver. Shirley hired Tony "Lip" Vallelonga, a waiter/bodyguard/bouncer who was out of work from his job at the famed New York Copacabana Night Club. The club was closing for two months for interior remodeling, so one of his customers hooked him up with the successful pianist, and the movie takes off. Tony was the iconic blue collar Italian, trying to make it in New York. The real Tony Lip did make it; he later had a part in "The Sopranos." His son, Nick Vallelonga has also had a successful acting and movie career, first appearing in the Godfather, a youngster as a wedding guest. He co-wrote the, "Green Book," screenplay, and co-produced it.

Tony and Don load up in one of two, aqua 1962 Cadillac Sedan Devilles and head south. The other identical Cadillac was used by the bassist and the cellist. The relationship between the tough Italian from the Bronx, and the stylish black piano virtuoso is portrayed on film with an excellence that contrasts favorably with, "Driving Miss Daisy." For my money, "Green Book," depicts the real nature of the American Human Condition. In a recent interview, Mahershala Ali paid Mortenson the best of compliments, "Thank you for making me better." Both of their characters passed away in 2013, always remaining close friends.

Our country's history of immigration has always treated the newcomers as threats. New Yorkers, from south Manhattan, looked down on just about everyone who couldn't pass as a white Anglo Saxon protestant. The Bronx, it may survive yet, was the home of the poor working class. It included Italians, the Irish, Blacks, Latinos, and other so-called minorities.

As a Texan with English, Scottish, and Irish ancestry, I never thought of myself or my friends as racist. When I look back at the school system in Corpus Christi, graduating from W.B. Ray in 1959, I never thought much about human physical differences. I believed MLK when he said we should be judged by our character and not by the color of our skin. I struggle more today, as an old white male, as I attempt to understand the division seeming to rack America's people with hatred. I think we all need to follow God's commandment, "To love our neighbors as we love ourselves."

CULTURE

DECEMBER 30, 2017
THE LIGHT WINS

MAY THE FORCE BE WITH YOU! I took my two young sons to see, "Star Wars," in 1977, and we loved it. Forty years later, and, "The Last Jedi," is hitting big numbers at the Christmas box office. My question for this post is: Has this entertainment series been positive for our culture? My answer is a definite yes. There are a few story lines I question, for example, Is Han Solo a drug runner? Gosh, I hope not. I'm curious about your thoughts. As a consumer of favorite movie characters, fun movies, fantastic visual effects, futuristic thinking, and philosophical messages, it scores an A+.

The first movie had characters both loved and hated, although those from the Dark Side did command a bit of misplaced respect. Come on, every young man would like to have a bit of Darth Vader in him. My favorite has always been Han Solo, a swashbuckling space traveler played by Harrison Ford. His sidekick, a 200 year old wookie, Chewbacca is a bit scary, but you can't fault his communication skills. As my grandsons became fans, I enjoyed trying to imitate him, and verbalizing uugghh, wwhhggaahhuugghghg usually meant, "Yes, we're going to get some ice cream."

The message, moral, and mythology of the film is Good winning over Evil. The mythology lessons center around the development of a real hero, Luke Skywalker, how he is supported and counseled by Obi Wan Kenobi, an aging Jedi Knight. He teaches Luke how to use the, "Force," for good, "The Light Side." This is somewhat biblical perhaps. John's gospel, Ch. 1, 4-5, "In him was life, and that life was the light of all mankind. The light shines in the darkness, and the darkness has not overcome it."

The creator, writer, and director, George Lucas, wanted to present kids in the 1970's the reality of a spiritual side of life. The tales of King Arthur and Beowulf inspired some of the cinematic and literary illusions. The knights of the Round Table, and the Jedi Knights both depended on their swords for defense and attack. Two of the most delightful characters were droids, R2D2, and C-3PO, who had amazing futuristic talents, but seem to argue back and forth like a couple of old maids. Film maker Lucas is a genius, but perhaps a greater risk taker. Back in 1977, his budget was $11 million, at the time quite a piece of change. It went on to be the most successful film series of all time. When you add in all the sequels, prequels, and merchandise, today, Disney has a $10 billion property. Although Lucas is forty years older, and the recent films in the series are written and directed by others his influence continues. We have not seen the last of "Star Wars." I haven't seen, "The Last Jedi," but so far the reviews have been pretty good, so I plan to buy a ticket. It will be fun to analyze and compare the new characters with the old.

Mark Hamil, Harrison Ford, and Alec Guiness will always be tough acts to follow. I'm sticking with Obi Wan Kenobi, "May the Force Be with Me!

DEC 2, 2017, 4:47 PM

RESPECT FOR THE LADIES

Have we run of the track, or is it just me? The news, or perhaps reporting the news, or maybe, the comments on those reporting the news have all gone awry. Draining the swamp is a bigger task than emptying the Pacific Ocean. How about this headline, "New smart condom, the icon, is about to hit the market." You don't want to go there.

Consider this one, "New colonies on the moon in five years." Some dreamer thinks we can develop lunar mining, and export product back to earth. In five years we'll be drilling in the Big Lunar Shale Formation, and piping cheap oil back to our refineries. There are loads of mind blowing headlines these days, but the worst of all are the reports of the elite sexual predators. I guess when we accepted the antics of Mr. William Jefferson Clinton in the Oval Office, and gave him a pass, things could only get worse. Yes, there are stories of past misbehaviors by power players in high places, but the man from Hope, Arkansas took it to a new level.

It seems like every day, we read about another male celeb making whoopee in or out of the office with an unsuspecting female. There aren't enough brooms to sweep all this stuff under the rug. Or maybe, there aren't enough rugs. We're on a cycle: going from bad to worse, going from worse to terrible, going from terrible to absolutely the worst ever.

I grew up in a time when females were ladies, and young men were taught to respect the fairer sex. Yes, back in the day, gentlemen opened doors for ladies, paid for dinner and the movie, and walked your date to the door. Those times have changed. I'm guilty, I've changed also. I still know what a gentlemen should do, but I'm not as respectful and gracious as I used to be, or I should be now. Today, we should consider the difference between gentlemen and ladies, and travel back in time when gallant behavior was appreciated.

Alas, I'm afraid there are no tracks wide enough to keep our degenerate culture from future ruin. But, let's not give up hope. So, the next time you have a chance to open a door for a female, don't waste the opportunity.

OCTOBER 14, 2017
BIGGER OR SMALLER

Lately, I feel like a voice crying in the wilderness. Mistakenly, I've believed flyover country is being skewered by the pomposity of the elite media, the dishonesty of the elected and appointed members of the bureaucratic government, the greed of the misplaced capitalistic drivers of the economy, and the degeneracy of the egotistical entertainment industry.

My research, such as it is, has led me to seek other voices crying in the wilderness. I have learned approximately 90% of our country's population live in urban areas, on about 5% of America's land area. The richest zip codes are found in overly populated metropolitan areas, and most of our more modest zip codes are occupied in small towns, close to the wonders of Americana's natural landscapes. The large majority of us appear to be content living our lives in and around the clogged, smogged, paved, potholed, congested, manufactured, zoned, restricted places we call cities. This seems out of necessity, as job opportunities are more plentiful.

One of the more insightful voices in the wilderness was the American naturalist and writer, Edward Abbey. Before he died in 1989, he wrote a neat little book, "A Voice Crying in the Wilderness." It is filled with thoughtful quotes, and a good dose of wisdom. Here are some of my favorites, "I come more and more to the conclusion that wilderness, in America or anywhere else, is the only thing left that is worth saving," and, "A patriot must always be ready to defend his country against government," and on the last page, "New Yorkers like to boast that if you can survive in New York, you can survive anywhere. But if you can survive anywhere, why live in New York?"

Now, down to the meat of things. If you want to live in a big city, you need to make a lot of money, pay a lot of taxes, and spend a good bit of time having bad days. Living in a small town, financial requirements are much less, taxes are less, crime is low, and you know who you do business with. There are lots of benefits to living small versus living large. Uninhabited areas are a lot closer, enabling you to cry loudly in the wilderness, and no one will hear you. The media, the government, the rich and powerful, and the degenerates will continue their immoral hedonistic lives. They wouldn't listen to your cries anyway. Living close to wilderness allows you to be deplorable, cry out, complain, or shout for joy. Plus, you won't be arrested by the local authorities for demonstrating without a permit.

JUL 29, 2017,

LOSING OUR GOD GIVEN RIGHTS

Never interrupt your enemy when he is making a mistake. Napoleon Bonaparte...Good advice when doing battle over 200 years ago as the Emperor didn't have the difficulties we have today figuring out who are our enemies. In fact, in truth by God, it seems it's a futile effort to identify real enemies and real friends. Napoleon got a bit mixed up after he met his Waterloo. His past friends became enemies, and exiled him to the island Saint Helena in the Atlantic Ocean.

Over two hundred years ago, big events seemed to bring folks together. America could use a big event. 9-11 brought us together for a time, but it didn't last. There are 325 million of us. We don't like each other. We don't trust each other. We don't have the freedoms we use to have. Today, if you exercise freedom of speech, you'll likely be called a racist, or maybe accused of a hate crime. We're taken to court if we exercise freedom of religion. The 10th Amendment protected our states' rights, but the courts have flipped that on us.

All of us are here either legally or illegally, but no

one seems to know who's who. We are 5% of the world's population, and 25% of the world's prison population. We're more afraid of the IRS than North Korea.

I cast my first vote for President in 1964. I valued my vote, and wanted to protect it. But, I was hoodwinked. I thought my vote counted for something, but those guys up in the District don't represent the people. Primarily, they represent themselves, and then their donors. They really like spending our money, for government largesse, and to hell with the people.

America is not just a country, it's an idea. Growing up after WWII, I believed we were the, "Land of the Free, and the Home of the Brave." Lately, it seems we're the, "land of the entitled, and the home of the elite." Our president acts as if he has many friends and many enemies. I think he interrupts his enemies when they make mistakes. At least I think Napoleon would have said so. I hope Mr. Trump does a good job for America, but his twitter account may turn into his Waterloo.

JUL 1, 2017, 5:20 PM
CONVENTION OF STATES

BANG! YOU'RE DEAD...These three words were used frequently by myself and my young friends, as we played "Cowboys and Indians," and "Cops and Robbers." We built forts in the back yard, and hid from each other in garages and behind fences. I always wanted to be one of the cowboys or a cop, but usually the older kids got to be the good guys.

If we played those games today, I'm sure we would be punished for our blatant political incorrectness. Do we think our neighborhood games have evolved into the real thing. Young boys in Chicago yell BANG! YOU'RE DEAD, and it's for real. Young actors would never dream of playing the part of an Indian, oops, I mean Native American. Are Chicago and Los Angeles destinations anymore? My son and I recently spent a week in New York City to watch the U.S. Open Tennis Tournament, played at Flushing Meadows in the borough of Queens. I had never spent any time in Queens, the home of our President, but there were lots of areas that reminded me of third world neighborhoods. No wonder President Trump comes across as a street fighter.

I know I'm a deplorable, but do we think our American

culture has made any real improvements over the past several decades. I must say the evolution, or perhaps devolution of our country's "Hoods," has been negative for many of our urban areas. Lately it's been easy to compare ancient Rome with our corrupt, "Inside the Beltway." Nine years ago, Cullen Murphy published, "Are We Rome?" A valid comparison?.....I wonder.

The Solution - The Convention of States. Please search for: conventionofstates.com. This grassroots project details the need for this movement. It is our only constitutional way to return power to the states, and to the people. The Federal Government is no longer, "Of, by, and for the people." Article V of the constitution gives us hope. The corrupt, inside the Beltway, parasitic elected members of Congress have led us to the edge of the cliff. I don't want to jump. Do you?

JUN 17, 2017,

MILITARY INDUSTRIAL COMPLEX

Are you sincerely concerned about our country, the United States of America? If not, I want to meet you. Lately my readings have led me to study the history of the late 20th century, and our 17 year old 21st century. Are we doomed if we don't learn the lessons of history? Now, there's a bit of food for thought!

Dwight D. Eisenhower has always been one of my heroes. Toward the end of his 2nd term as President, he warned us about the growth of the Military Industrial Complex. I remember I didn't seem too concerned as I was fresh out of high school, and "Military," and "Industry," were the two major factors enabling us and our allies to win WWII.

Today, I'm beginning to see the wisdom of Ike's warning. I'm pretty sure our Military strength was the difference in winning the, "Cold War." I'm pretty sure even V. Putin would agree Stalin was a monster. But post 1989, having won the Cold War, did we help Russia become an ally in the same vein as our support of Japan and Germany? Back then, I thought with Boris Yeltsin, we had a chance. But, no more.

Our Military Industrial Complex is alive and well. Who, exactly, profits from our giant corporations? Is it the people? No, it's our pork laden federal government, our greedy casinos on Wall Street, and our ego driven celebrities in Hollywood?

I think I'm destined to be a deplorable, living in flyover country, and doing my best to love my neighbors, but having trouble loving my enemies. I'm not sure who they are.

APR 23, 2017,

FUTURE EVOLUTION?

Yesterday's history, tomorrow's a mystery, and today is what's happening. I'm paraphrasing here, but since I don't know who coined the first expression, I'm unable to give credit. Man has always wanted to learn more about his past, and many have spent lifetimes predicting the future. I'm a student of history, and would love to predict the future, but after many decades, those two endeavors have not helped me pay the bills.

Like many of you, I find myself on the internet before my day gets started. I usually check my email, go to my favorites list, and try to gain some sense of what is going on in our world. Frequently, my curiosity takes me to sites I've never been, and when my speed reading slows to a crawl, I settle in on a topic that piques my interest. By then, it's already time for me to get going on more pressing things than electronic surfing. Hopefully I will return later to continue down the current rabbit hole. This week, it's been AI, Artificial Intelligence, think super computers that think for themselves. This brings us to the, "Singularity." Now there's a term to get your attention.

OLD WHITE MAN

Singularity is defined as the outcome of the human brain merging with Artificial Intelligence. I refer you to two scientist/inventors, Elon Musk and Ray Kurzweil. Both are over the top when it comes to acting on future predictions. I don't believe their prototypes will be ready for the masses until my time here is over; however, our children and grandchildren need to be ready. The future of humanity may be the next major development in the evolution of man. The term, cyborg, connotes a combination of humanity in its present form, and augmented with additional artificial intelligence. If this occurs, it must be part of God's work. If the future inhabitants of earth are more advanced than we are, I'm sure we will still need to call on Jesus Christ for our salvation.

In an article, recently published in the "Atlantic," Jonathan Merritt wrote of the possible relationships between Artificial Intelligence and theology. I posted it to Facebook. It posed hard questions when it comes to my Christianity. The Singularity and its future prospects could have an impact as significant as Darwin's, "Origin of the Species."

I'm praying that our Father will continue to love us and keep us, and guide us to be disciples for Jesus Christ. And for good measure, I'll include the Serenity Prayer. KEEP THE FAITH!

NOVEMBER 24, 2018
FAITH IS IN DECLINE

Did Curiosity really kill the cat? My curiosity won't kill me, but it seems to confirm a significant lack of knowledge. Perhaps the more I study, the closer I will come to learning the value of keeping my mouth shut. I often spend time searching for meaning, meaning about lots of things. It is frustrating to think, just another Google click and I'll get it. Should we worry about the transfer of all things to digital cloud storage? If so, will nostalgia lose its significance?

Is it too soon to think about 2019 resolutions? I'm definitely including the need to keep my mouth shut, as well as a desire to eliminate worrying about just about everything. Worrying is a hard habit to control. Not only am I worrying about next Saturday's game against Oklahoma, I've already begun thinking about the 2020 presidential election. I've just now committed to a, "What, me worry?" attitude toward all things political for a New Year's resolution.

I'll try and leave politics out of the rest of this post. So, what about religion? Is it in decline? In as much as all religions believe in something greater than man, the trend today is an increase in humanism, and a decline in a belief in the supernatural. This has had an effect at every level, and in all connections.

You can google up, "Decline in religion," "Decline in Christianity," or "Decline in faith." You name it. You'll have enough articles to last you till Christmas. By the way, I hope all had a Happy Thanksgiving. How did we make it before deep fried turkey?

Several years ago, I read a lengthy two volume book, "The Story of Christianity," by Justo L Gonzalez, a retired Ph.D. in historical theology from Yale University. Dr. Gonzalez discusses the crisis of Christian faith in Europe and the United States, but is optimistic concerning the growth of Christianity in Africa, Asia, and South America. My logic leads me to believe as materialism thrives, faith begins to lose its perceived value as well as its real value.

As Christians we have lost our way in sharing the gospel. We have tried to debate God's Creation with the Earth's Evolution. There is nothing about evolution that threatens the reality of God or his son, Jesus Christ. Read these words from the book of Genesis: "In the beginning, God created the heavens and the earth. Now, the earth was formless and empty, darkness was over the surface of the deep, and the Spirit of God was hovering over the waters." I don't believe Darwin could argue with this statement. These words were written 3500 years ago. Some folks just can't wrap their arms around the concept of a, "Beginning."

One lesson from all the great faiths of the world is "Unconditional Love." The command to love our neighbor is from a faith in something greater than ourselves. It is only with the knowledge of a loving God that I am able to not only accept all of humankind, but to try and want the best for all of humanity. We will not conquer evil until love conquers us. The gospel allows us to accept ourselves with all our weaknesses. Without God, there is no meaning to life; there is only existence.

A United Methodist pastor once told me, all humanity is trying to connect with the same hardware, a loving God. Us Methodists use a little different software package to help us get there. We all yearn for something greater than ourselves. I'm praying your software is debugged and making great connections with your hardware.

OCTOBER 27, 2018
$0.25 OR $25

A friend and I just returned from San Antonio, and there's not a lot of time till the Longhorn game. I'm sure my post will be difficult as my mind will be trying to focus on college football. Texas hasn't had this good a start in several football seasons, so right now I'm getting motivated for a good game, and hopefully a 7th straight win.

On our drive back down I37 we got to talking about heroes. Both of us agreed that our first heroes were our fathers. When I turned one year old, my Dad was in the army, and on his way to North Africa. My sister and I lived with our mother, and our two grandparents during the World War II years. I will always remember a framed picture of our father, in his army officer uniform, which was placed on a small table that I passed by every time I came downstairs, and headed to the kitchen. The soldier in the picture, my Dad, was my hero, and when I was five, I got to meet him in the flesh. He was the same man in the picture, and right away, I knew he was special.

As I grew older, I got some more heroes. I remember going to the Tower Movie Theatre every Saturday morning.

For a quarter, you could get a ticket to the movie, a coke, and a bag of popcorn. The movie included a cartoon, a serial, and a feature movie. Roy Rogers was my favorite. His horse, Trigger, was the prettiest palomino stallion ever, and the supporting cast was the best. I grew up loving western movies, and I still do today.

I saw my first John Wayne movie on one of those Saturday mornings. He soon replaced all the others, and I have been a John Wayne fan for life. Although he died when I was thirty-eight, I have continued to enjoy his movies. I bet I've watched Rio Bravo over fifty times. If I'm right, that's about a hundred hours and fifty popcorn bags of movie enjoyment; easily worth the price increase to more than $25. The film also starred Walter Brennan, Dean Martin, and Ricky Nelson. All four stars have passed on, so maybe I'll get to meet them sometime down the trail.

The Western movie genre has always been the best for my money. John Wayne fit the role better than anyone. It didn't matter if he played the Sheriff, the Calvary Officer, the Big Rancher, the Fast Gun, or the old, hard drinking, one eyed Rooster Cogburn, he was the best. One of John Wayne's best quotes, was "I do think we have a pretty wonderful country, and I thank God that He chose me to live here." I'm praying hard America can get back to being that wonderful country John Wayne loved.

OCTOBER 20, 2018
TRIBAL POLARIZATION

Ever play that word association game? If someone says, "Tribe," I think, "Comanche." A tribe, historically, has been a defined group of people with a unifying set of beliefs. Beliefs don't sit well with other tribes. Today, the term has been hijacked by the news media, frequently criticizing political parties as being tribal. Bringing tribalism into the political discourse, would lead one to believe the different parties are at war with each other. This was not what our founders intended. The Constitution was written with the intent that tribes or factions would not be shut out by the majority.

Our Congress used to operate with one political party in the majority, and the other, the "Loyal Opposition." This relationship enabled all to have a voice. Federalist 10, written by James Madison, had the intent that the elected members of Government would be acting toward the common good. There was an initial American value that all people would be considered when laws were made. We wouldn't be a bunch of tribes always fighting with each other, but 13 states, operating with equal rights, and separate governments, but all of us united with the values of life, liberty, and the pursuit of happiness, therefore, loyal to the Constitution. We would be the United States, OK?

My research for this week's post led me to a source entitled, "Hidden Tribes: A Study of America's Polarized Landscape." The study was conducted by, "More in Common," an initiative with a goal of getting us more united. Their findings were informative. They differentiated voters from the far left to the far right. The far left is 8% of the sample, and the far right is 6%. That's less than 15% of the total.

Why does the News concentrate on this small percent? Most of us are in the big middle. We don't spend our time protesting, rioting, demonstrating, complaining, or fighting. Faith, family, vocation, and community occupy our time. Unfortunately, we now have the 24-hour news cycle, and the unchecked Internet.

The continual storms of, "Breaking News," are flooding us with often meaningless information. The really important news is frequently overlooked, or minimalized by stories which have little impact on us, stressing the billion dollar lottery or the two headed alligator removed from a Florida golf course. Lately, we see the decline in our culture and common decency. Get a TV camera out there with the Antifa and the Proud Boys, and you will be either entertained or annoyed, depending on who gets the last invective.

If you're concerned about climate change, that's ok with me. Just don't try and keep me from enjoying low energy costs.

COLLEGIALITY AMONG THE SWAMP RATS

Hookem! The Longhorns notched another win.

Kavanaugh, Kagan, and Kennedy, three jurists with character, disagreements, and close friendships. Wouldn't it be nice for the rest of the folks in our government to work with each other with a goal of unity and compromise.

Judge Kavanaugh clerked for Justice Kennedy when he sat on the Supreme Court. Current Supreme Court Justice Kagan, was once the Dean of the Harvard Law School. She hired Judge Kavanaugh to be a professor of Constitutional Law.

I'm sure retired Justice Kennedy would be proud for one of his law clerks to be named to the bench of the highest court in the land. I'm sure Justice Kagan would welcome Judge Brett Kavanaugh as an associate justice on the court.

Victor Davis Hanson just wrote an article discussing how close the United States is to a pre-Civil War mentality. The Media, the intellectually elite, the entertainment celebs, the corporate elite, and most evident, the prevaricators in the Deep State and the Swamp rats inside the Beltway, all are taking us, the people, down. When we all learn that America was founded on, "Equal Justice for All," not social justice for those selected by the government. Justice is not social. It is Justice, period.

APRIL 21, 2018
PRISON MINISTRY

"Amazing Grace," what a song, what a poem. We sang this wonderful hymn, Thursday, behind the walls of the Connally Unit, a Texas Maximum Security Prison. The song was also sung today during the funeral service for Barbara Bush, our First Lady during the Presidential term of her husband, George Herbert Walker Bush.

Immediately, I considered the vast differences between the small prison chapel, and the immense, beautiful interior of St. Martin's Episcopal Church in Houston. "Amazing Grace," an English hymn was written by John Newton, an English ship captain, who for a time made his living as a slave trader. During this period, he almost lost his ship and his life, but fortunately was able to make it safely to the Irish shore. The experience led him back to Christianity, and after a few more years at sea, returned to England and became a Christian Pastor. Some say the words, "Amazing Grace saved a wretch like me," referred to his sinful life as a slave trader.

Somehow, I see a connection between the trappings of St. Martin's Church and the sparse Prison Chapel. I know

Barbara Bush believed in the Grace of our Lord Jesus Christ. She lived a beautiful life, and it would have been her choice that slave traders never would have existed. But, it was what it was. One of our country's founding values is liberty, and it was wrong for one man to own another. But slavery had been practiced since the dawn of humanity, so it has been a struggle for us as a people to eliminate not only slavery, but the results of slavery.

As we sang, "Amazing Grace," in the Prison Chapel, I was standing between two descendants of black slaves, who may have been brought to the new world by John Newton. We never ask them about their crime or their sentence, but I know life behind bars is more than punishment. I won't deny our efforts as a people to improve human rights, not only in Texas prisons, but all across the globe. But much is still needed to be done. There are many men in the Connally Unit who have accepted Christ, and I know when they meet their maker, they will arrive in the same place Barbara Bush is right now. And they will get a chance to meet John Newton, and thank him for the words to a favorite hymn, "Amazing Grace."

JANUARY 27, 2018
FUTURE LEADERS

What a show! The 83rd Annual Nueces County Junior
Livestock Show. Down here in South Texas, in flyover
country, from January 8 through January 20, 2018, after
months of preparation, Nueces County won the Blue Ribbon.
Over 5,000 youth, family, friends, volunteers, caterers,
committee members, educators, project judges, agricultural
professionals, auction buyers, representatives from many
local businesses, and many more good South Texas folks
enjoyed another special time when the county puts on its
best, and gives all of us priceless moments to cherish forever.

Three youth organizations come together, compete, and
members congratulate each other with every ribbon won. 4H
Clubs have been supporting youth for over a hundred years.
It's the largest youth development organization in the world,
with over 7 million members, from the age of 6 to 26. Head,
Heart, Hands, and Health, represented with an H on each
leaf of a four leaf clover is the iconic emblem of each club.
500,000 volunteers, and over 100 public universities are
involved with the 4H mission supporting youth's education
and involvement with the agricultural industry.

FFA is another youth organization which is well represented. FFA, Future Farmers of America, chapters are primarily represented at the high school level. The organization includes over five hundred thousand members with chapters in every state in the country. A positive result from FFA is the flexibility they offer to a kid to get involved, raising an animal, in a high school facility. Most residences in the city aren't equipped with a goat or lamb pen. You can always spot an FFA member wearing his or her dark blue jacket with the bright yellow FFA seal on the back.

Somewhat new to the show are members of the FCCLA. The letters stand for Family, Career and Community Leaders of America. This organization also is represented at the high school level. Several area high schools have FCCLA chapters, and they bring a number of new consumer projects to the show.

Farming and ranching are part of the American DNA. While we have witnessed the decline in the American Cowboy, and the American family farm, we are enjoying the greatest agricultural industry ever. Youth who participate are prepared for just about any field of endeavor as young adults.

In 2005, a country singer, Jason Aldean recorded a song, "Amarillo Sky." It's about a farmer plowing his fields in the hot Texas sun. As he drives his tractor, he sends up another prayer, "Lord, I never complain, never ask why, please don't let my dreams run dry, underneath, underneath this Amarillo Sky."

JANUARY 20, 2018
GETTING READY IN THE HEARTLAND

The week got me. Horseshow last Sunday, cataract surgery Tuesday, and today, a large dose of Americana; the Nueces County Junior Livestock Show. I've already bought a lamb, and have to return soon to bid on a goat. The two grandsons have done a great job with their 4H projects, and us Grandparents want to follow their success.

The Blue-Ribbon Show and Auction gets started with our National Anthem. This year our middle grandson sang it, solo. I teared up. For us grandparents, it was the greatest rendition we've ever heard, and I know Francis Scott Keys would have been proud.

Look forward to posting again next Saturday.

MAY 19, 2019
ARE YOU MY NEIGHBOR?

Where are we right now? I'm referring to the United States of America, Land of the Free, and Home of the Brave, May 19, 2019. There are 325 million of us. Who are we, and where are we going? Important questions, don't you think.

I just finished reading, "The Second World Wars," by Victor Davis Hanson. Wars is plural as almost every nation in the world took a side. Only ten countries were able to maintain neutrality. Over 70 million soldiers and civilians lost their lives, at a time when world population was 2.3 billion. At the end of the war, America took its place as the leader of the free world.

Today, our leadership is in jeopardy. This past week I watched the timeless western, "The Good, the Bad, and the Ugly." I'm going to jump out on a limb, and call us the Good, the Bad, and the Ugly. How the heck do I use a Clint Eastwood, Italian Western, to connect with us folks today? Perhaps, I need a flashback to World War II.

The major combatants were the Axis powers, Germany, Japan, and Italy, lined up against the Allies, USA, Great

Britain, and the Soviet Union. The war produced a number of, "Goods, Bads, and Uglies." The Allies were the good guys, and the Axis were the bad guys. At least that's how I see it. There were many uglies, who for the most part, mixed in with both sides.

Here's a few examples: General George Patton was definitely a Good. He was like the wild west hero who comes in and cleans up a town, but then the townspeople want him to move on. Germany's General Erwin Rommel was a Bad. He's like the wild west gun hand who comes in and takes over a town, and the folks can't get rid of him. Then there's Russia's General Grigory Ivanovich Kulik who was an ugly. He's like the wild west bandit who comes into town and makes a menace of himself.

In the movie, Clint Eastwood, "Blondie," was the GOOD. Lee Van Cleef, "Angel Eyes," was the BAD, and Eli Wallach, "Tuco," was the UGLY. Eastwood did not play a part matching up with the all-time greatest, John Wayne. No one can compare with the Duke. Blondie was a good guy, but on the wrong side of the law. You might say Patton was on the wrong side of the Supreme Allied Command. Van Cleef was a bad guy who didn't much care if he killed anyone who was in his way, but he did carry himself with class and respect. Rommel was a great warrior, but he lined himself up with the most evil Dictator of the 20th century. Now, Wallach was the epitome of ugly. He was dirty, unkempt, sloppy, greedy, and a cloud of evil was always around him. Kulik was an ineffective Russian general, often referred to as a murderous buffoon. After the war, Stalin had him executed for treason.

So….We get to us. How do we retain our position as the free world leader, a charitable nation, always lending our resources to those in need, both here and abroad. We won't get there as the Good, the Bad, and the Ugly. No, we need a better reality. Where are the coastal elites in a, "Better reality? Where does the media fit? What about the politicians? How do we rid ourselves us of the constant bickering? You would think we all want a part in the movie.

We need to be Americans again. We need honesty in everything. We need fairness. We need to respect and follow the law. This is a tall, and I mean a really, tall order. Mr. Rogers is gone. But he gave us a great message for a better reality. He told us we need to be neighbors, really good neighbors.

Will YOU be my NEIGHBOR?

MAY 4, 2019

DIGNITY ANYONE?

Do you remember, "Dragnet?" What a great radio/TV show, starring Jack Webb, as Detective Friday. Here's a homeless take using the, "Dun Du Dun dun, DuuUUNNNN! Only the names have been changed to protect the innocent." My program director's name is Joe. My name is Thursday, and I was getting ready to facilitate the Tuesday morning group counseling session. We operate a drug and alcohol treatment center for court ordered felons.

I got a call from one of our admin.asst's, who reported Billy, one of our clients was already in the group room, thirty minutes early, asleep on the floor. I went in to see about him. He had been beaten badly, and his clothes were torn. Able to wake him, and usher him into my office, I began to find out what had happened. He told me he wasn't allowed to stay in his homeless shelter due to a failed urine analysis for alcohol.

He had spent the night in a city park, and during the night, he was awakened, being beaten by several men, who then stole his coat and his wallet. Luckily, he still had his SSI Debit card in his front pocket, but wouldn't get his monthly allotment for another week. I'll get back to Billy, but I want to share some facts, numbers, ideas, and opinions about our problem of homelessness.

Homelessness; what are the causes? Is it inequality of incomes? Is it the lack of affordable housing? Is it the increased use of alcohol and drugs? Is it past trauma and resulting mental issues? These are all factors, but the root cause begins to grow early in life. Society and culture are always in flux. Sometimes, things are getting better, and other times life is more of a struggle. Today, May 4, 2019, Mother Earth and people everywhere are spinning out of control. Technological change is breaking the sound barrier. Families are in freefall. Dysfunction is spreading like kudzu. Making it to age 25 is like a walk in Jumanji. If you make it on your own, no major debt, and on your way to a rewarding career, you deserve, "Congratulations!"

If you don't have a home or an apartment to sleep in tonight, you are 1 of over 500 thousand persons in America. Just 1 is too many. Down here in Corpus Christi, Texas, on the southern edges of Flyover Country, there are 424 persons, at last count, who don't have a home. Most days there are enough available beds to serve those in need, but the reality for many is a night on the streets. These unfortunates have lost respect, dignity, pride, not to mention the where-with-all to make it in today's environment. The causes and reasons are many and complex. Life starts as a miracle, a dependent infant, a special child of God. Without a daily dose of unconditional love, and best efforts of a loving support group, the child begins to struggle. By adolescence, choices become misfires, outcomes are in doubt.

The intellectually honest professionals all recognize the negative changes in many family structures. We all know families are failing. The intellectually elite would have us believe differently. It's because of racism, corporate greed, income inequality, hate, lack of adequate public funds, and victimhood.

The amount of public funds directed at the homeless problem is difficult to determine. I like to pick on California. I don't know if it's my love of Texas, or my disgust with Hollywood, but I have dug up some dirt on Los Angeles and San Francisco. Federal and state money is directed at the homeless in both of these high dollar big cities. This past year, their local governments threw $1.5 billion at a homeless population of over 50,000. That's $30,000 for every man, woman, and child living homeless in those two cities.

The problem is getting worse. THAT'S UNACCEPTABLE!

The new family member for these people is a free cell phone, and the new drug is an electric outlet. Outrageous!

Back to our client, Billy. Billy is over 50. His last real job was an eighteen wheel trucker. He became addicted to meth to keep him awake, and alcohol to put him to sleep. He's been locked up a number of times. He recently completed a six month residence in a state Substance Abuse Felony Punishment facility, and a three month residence in a local state approved halfway house. At our treatment facility we provide outpatient treatment for several months, with a hope, the client will complete major life changes.

Billy was relocated to a second-floor duplex for four men, each with a monthly payment of $150. After several months, the owner of the duplex gave Billy the title of house manager. He successfully completed his outpatient treatment. When he received his completion certificate, he was smiling and sober as a judge. I don't know his status today, but I have a glimmer of hope; he has regained some lost respect, dignity, and pride.

APRIL 27, 2019

WOKEN, BLOKEN, AND NOD

Are you woke? I've been hearing this term, and did a bit of internet research to learn more. The derivation of woke is from African American Vernacular English, from the question, "Are you awake?" The answer is, "I'm woke." If you're woke today, it means you are socially aware. Here's a couple of examples: "Are you going to the Black Lives Matter demonstration today? No, I'm not woke." "What do you think of Kamala Harris? Man, she's woke." Personally, I don't like the word. I think it's demeaning to people of color. The Woke Fokes must believe they are in the know. Slang may be cool, but it is not an indicator of intelligence. If you're shooting baskets, and drinking beer afterward, then a little slang may be appropriate.

If, on the other hand you are an activist with Black Lives Matter, you can make your point with better use of the King's English. When you listen to Congressional members of the Black Caucus, the most influential are those who use excellent English. My opinion is woke is hokey. It's a step backward. Barbara Jordan is turning over in her grave listening to African American Vernacular English. Do you remember the success of Ebonics? African Americans working on real success recognized the futility of trying to use Black Slang. As an old white man, I would much rather listen to Charlie Pride sing, than Snoop Dog rap.

Do you use memes? Now, there's another word that has lost its original meaning. A meme is, "a popular idea, saying, or description, which spreads within a culture." A good example is, "sandwich." The Earl of Sandwich put a piece of ham between some bread, and it became a meme. The word has taken on a different meaning of late. It's basically a word, idea, video, phrase, having gone viral on the internet. Click on, "Honey Badger," or a YouTube with thousands of hits, and you've found a couple of memes. The meme, sandwich, has stood the test of time. I doubt the honey badger will be here next year.

Another word which could be a meme, and it could be woke is, "Screen Time." We used to think of screen time as how much time a movie actor spent on the screen. "He was so bad, they shouldn't have given him so much screen time." Or, "She was so good looking, she should have gotten more screen time." The term has been hijacked by the cell phone woke fokes. Now, "Screen Time," is how much time you spent looking at your cell phone screen. I'm trying to spend less screen time. How about you?

If you're woke, live in a meme world, use a lot of screen time you may be socially aware of the homeless problem we have in our country. Did you know over 550 thousand people are counted as homeless. Over 20% of them are in California. I could write 100 Saturday evening posts, and couldn't approach this sad reality. I wonder if the woke fokes are concerned about this national disgrace?

APRIL 7, 2019
PRISON MINISTRY

KAIROS Prison Ministry International depends on over 30,000 volunteers who bring the presence of God, and his love for offenders, into 500 prisons in 37 states and 9 countries.

The United States is the world's leader in incarceration with 2.3 million people currently in the nation's prisons or jails, a 500% increase over the past thirty years. Recently, the Congress Passed the First Step Act, and my hope, it is just a first step. The law applies to the Federal Prison System. Hopefully, states will follow suit with similar prison reform legislation.

Without quoting the legislation, the intent is to provide for increased fairness in sentencing, provide for improved rehabilitation and education, and reduce recidivism. The law originated with the White House, and garnered the unlikely support of Trump, Kanye West, the Kardashians, and the ACLU. It was passed by both houses of Congress on a bi-partisan basis.

The John B. Connally unit is a maximum security prison for men in Kenedy, Texas. KAIROS initiated its ministry there in 2002. At the time, the unit had the reputation of one of the toughest prisons in the state. A willing KAIROS volunteer and a courageous offender in the unit began work to bring the Christian ministry into the unit. Yesterday, KAIROS celebrated its 32nd four day retreat, and it was glorious. After each retreat, volunteers continue to support and attend weekly and monthly programs in the unit. The four day retreats are scheduled twice during the year.

In addition to KAIROS, several other volunteer organizations have brought positive programs into the unit. It is well-known how prisoner attitudes and morale, along with similar changes in the correctional staff have improved over the past several years. It is also evident the recidivism rate has declined significantly.

In most prison environments, the offenders have a tendency to segregate themselves. When KAIROS puts on an event, segregation disappears and integration blooms. Hispanics, whites, blacks, Asians; all find new relationships with each other. After approximately 35 hours of fellowship, meal sharing, singing, praying, laughing, and listening, real change takes place. Lives are changed.

With continued prison reform, faith based volunteer programs, and improved rehabilitation efforts, one of our country's systems is going in the right direction.

Much is wrong in our country. Many of our institutions are failing because our people have ceased to be in community with each other. The partisanship in local, state, and national political subdivisions is toxic. I'm an old, white male, and I don't remember a time when there has been such mistrust, such lack of cooperation, and such inability to reach out to one another.

I don't intend to reread, "Brave New World," or, "1984." Huxley and Orwell were wrong. Their pessimism is not welcome in the U.S.A. However, we have been warned by real history. Both George Santayana and Winston Churchill are credited with the quote, "Those who fail to learn from history, are doomed to repeat it." Many have been put to the test by radicals trying to change the powers of government. Most of the time a radical will fail. The last truly radical man who met with great success was the King himself, Jesus Christ of Nazareth.

MARCH 16, 2019
PRIVILEGE LOST

ANCIENT CHINESE WISDOM FROM CONFUCIUS: "When words lose their meaning, people lose their freedom." I'm an old white male, and I worry about my constitutional freedoms.

If you grew up in Flyover Country, in the Heartland of America, you knew the meaning of freedom. Most likely it was burned into you. The history of our country was revered. We were grateful for the blessings of this wonderful, "Land of the free, and the home of the brave." If your ancestors came from Western Europe, they came here for a new and better opportunity for life, liberty, and the pursuit of happiness.

After defeating the evils of Hitler's Third Reich, and Hirohito's Imperial Japan, America began to understand its moral fiber, and its yearning for real peace through strength. During the 1950's and 60's the United States took steps to insure real equality for all its people. We rightly recognized our own weaknesses as we wept for the tragic deaths of JFK and MLK. We outlasted the totalitarian Union of Soviet Socialist Republics. In 1989 the Berlin Wall came tumbling down. I pray for the day we will no longer need a barrier on our southern border.

It has taken just thirty years for the greatest country in the history of the world to lose its way. Our, "Great Society," with noble intentions, lit the hidden flame of high taxes and low morals. History tells us they are always precursors to the decline in all once, great nations. Our bastions of higher learning, the centers for the free exchange of ideas, have become crowded with thought police, rude behavior, and meaningless demonstrations.

I am saddened by the distrust, the misinformation, the downright cheating taking place by so many who think a diploma is something to be bought, and not earned. It seems like every day, I hear someone, often myself, say, "What has happened to us?" or, "Have we lost our minds?" I don't know about you, but I don't think we're ready for a one world order. We pay to train the Afghanistan police, while a sheriff in Kentucky can't get the funds to keep his county safe. One third of teenagers admitted to emergency rooms are suicidal, yet we spend millions on protecting illegal aliens. I'm sorry, that's undocumented asylum seekers.

I started this rant complaining. I'm concerned that words are losing their meaning. Being politically correct is more important than telling the truth. I suggest you go to the Facebook page, "Political Correctness Gone Wild." Read about, "All white Christians are terrorists." Double talk ain't what it used to be. If someone says, "Howdy," they may be perceived as a phony, when they're really just a good ole deplorable from Flyover Country.

I want to bring back, "Baseball, hot dogs, Mom, and Apple Pie." I want to watch my grandson and his teammates, led by his coach in prayer after the game, win or lose. Looking at a field of bluebonnets, red Indian paintbrush, and white wild thistles still stir a feeling of gratitude for our freedoms. I worry we have forgotten, our freedom isn't free. It was paid for over and over by brave men and women.

You know what they say about those old white males. They never die, just lose their privilege.

THE OLD RUGGED CROSS

Second trip to the, "Empty Cross, The Resurrection, The Way, The Strong Tower, The Narrow Gate, The Light, The Mighty Fortress, The Door." Wow! My first visit, I was by myself. Today, I was joined by my bride, of over thirty years, and our beautiful granddaughter. Our drive to San Antonio was foggy and cloudy, but as we neared Kerrville, the sun came out, and the weather was delightful.

As we walked the paths of the beautiful, "The Coming King Sculpture Prayer Garden," we experienced its purpose; to bring hope, peace, joy and blessings to visitors, and at the same time, to bring glory and honor to Jesus Christ. Sometimes I feel the need to end my posts, which often point out dilemmas facing our world, with a message of needing to love our neighbors. Today, I've begun with an image giving us real motivation to follow this commandment.

We need more days like we had this February 16, 2019. Politics and fake news were not on our minds. The beautiful bluebonnets and Indian paintbrush, blooming along the Interstate, let us experience the first days of spring, which won't show up on the calendar for another month.

OLD WHITE MAN

If you're as old as me, you might be working on your bucket list. The overpowering Empty Cross, the focal point of the beautiful sculpture garden, is a must. If you know when you've pinched yourself, you will surely experience a special time. Driving from San Antonio, as you reach your first exit into Kerrville, you can see the Cross on a hill at the Northwest corner of I10 and HWY 16. The actual address is 520 Benson, in Kerrville.

The next time you find yourself in the Texas Hill Country, try to include this special place on your itinerary. I promise you, you will want to return.

JANUARY 19, 2019
WHOA-MEN

TOXIC MASCULINITY, Leave my male chauvinism alone! JANUHAIRY; it's your bodies, ladies, go for it. Does anyone have a remote idea why the most advanced society in the history of the world has been highjacked by the, "Thought Police?" Have we reached this zenith in science, information technology, advanced communication, and space exploration, but lost all common sense.

First, with deference to the fairer sex, let us examine the celebration of female hairiness, a movement started in Great Britain to exhibit the follicle side of feminism. I kid you not. This has gone viral. At first I was O.K. with the sudden trend. But I soon learned the purpose was to raise funds for an organization with the title, "Body Gossip." This forward thinking group educates children to explore their bodies and gain insight into all of the LGBT possibilities for the future. I'm sure the psychology profession is gleeful just thinking about all the fees to be generated by this new snowflake generation.

Now, let's turn our attention to the predator side of the male sex. In the past, men were hunters, breadwinners, protectors, warriors, and spear throwers. Now we must get in touch with our feminine side. It seems these same psychologists are concerned about toxic masculinity. Taken literally, were on the same level as a male rattlesnake.

Perhaps you have heard about or seen the new Gillette commercial, supposedly getting men to recognize their soft skin. Yes, this is the same corporate giant which shares its name with the stadium where the New England Patriots play professional football. These men grow beards and long hair, paint their faces with black swooshes, wear body armor, helmets with facemasks, and like to run full speed into another player, tackle him, and bring him down to the turf. And by gosh, it's great entertainment for a large percentage of the population. The women of New England proudly wear the red, white, and blue jerseys of their favorite players. I believe they adore these real pros, toxic masculinity or not.

Well, let's see. As I gaze out at the American Heartland, here in southern Flyover Country, I think we'll be O.K. I don't worry about a renewal of the Bearded Lady from the circus, and I'm not worried about contact sports losing its flair. The real fans are watching football all over the country. Fathers are teaching sons the techniques and fundamentals of football, with pads and helmets for protection. Ice hockey is alive and well; dropping the gloves, and going at it, will still get you five minutes in the penalty box.

We still appreciate beauty pageants, Hollywood Queens, and cheerleaders. I haven't noticed any Golden

Globes or Academy Awards going to lovely actresses with hairy legs. Yes, it might come to that, but for now, I'm pretty secure; BOYS WILL BE BOYS, and thanks for the fairer sex, GIRLS WILL GET OUR ATTENTION!

JANUARY 12, 2019
PROMISED LAND?

Hello, Walls
How'd things go for you today?
Miss Pelosi
You just up and walked away.
I bet you're smiling happy, and feelin nice
and free,
But lonely walls, won't keep you company.
Hello Borders,
Looks like you're open every mile
All the folks are comin
To our country and they'll stay awhile.
Don't call Chuck, he's got no sense
He just forgot he voted for a fence.
Hello Checkpoint
Well I see that you're still here
Catch some illegals?
Guess we've got nothing to fear.
Now look here, I bet you've got a Kilo
Stashed away somewhere,

soon you'll go down the road without a single care.

Hello, Walls

We need you standing tall

Hey Mr. POTUS

Things are just about to fall.

We've gotta all stick together, or else I'll lose my mind.

I think this crisis will last a long, long time. Thank you, Mr. Willie Hugh Nelson! Native Texan, living in Flyover Country, and working to make America the Heartland again.

HISTORY

OCT 28, 2017, 4:34 PM
AMERICAN GOODNESS

Please don't let me go down another rabbit hole. I've been studying the French aristocrat, Alexis De Tocqueville and his opinions about American culture, politics, racism, philosophy, and other facets of our democratic republic, as he found it during the 1820's. As I read more about his perspective on America's early way of life, it becomes harder and harder to figure out how we ever made it to here.

Chasing down the rabbit hole, or perhaps, jumping into the briar patch, are often the result of picking a subject, and finding how scant is one's knowledge of it. De Tocqueville found many positives about our young, growing country, still just a babe, rocked with care by the likes of Betsy Ross and Dolly Madison. But we were growing up fast, with an adolescent wildness hard to tame. I wonder if the many, mounted, and armed so-called raiders, fighting for or against, state or union sovereignty, even knew the meaning of the words.

As we approached the Civil War, we found the real meaning of an oxymoron. There was no civility to be found. As an honest broker, I believe both the Union, and the Confederacy had cause. The Union found the South an upstart band of rebels, and the South believed it was fighting for its independence. After the idiocy of war, Generals Grant and Lee displayed amazing respect for each other, and both regretted the carnage of their armies.

Surfing around with my friend Dell, we found a forgotten De Tocqueville quote, "I sought for the greatness and genius of America in her commodious harbors and her ample rivers, and it was not there...in her fertile fields and boundless forests, and it was not there...in her rich mines and her vast world commerce, and it was not there...in her democratic Congress and her matchless Constitution...and it was not there. Not until I went into the churches of America and heard her pulpits aflame with righteousness, did I understand the secret of her genius and power. America is great because she is good, and if America ever ceases to be good, she will cease to be great."

MARCH 24, 2017

DEVOLUTION OF DEMOCRACY

My mind is working hard to control feelings of anger. Once again, our government is unable to respond to the people. Our elected officials would rather engage each other with lofty, but meaningless rhetoric. Any piece of legislature is too complicated for even the most talented and overpaid bureaucrat to understand. President Trump is not the perfect President. There never has been one. Even with his faults, he has been working harder than any President in my lifetime. My first Presidential vote went to Goldwater. I have voted in every election since; won some...lost some. As I look back, I'm always reminded of Charles Dicken's, Tale of Two Cities. The opening lines of his novel, written about the French Revolution, were, "It is the best of times, and the worst of times." 2017 isn't any different. I think it's time to start over. Democracy isn't democracy. Capitalism isn't capitalism. Socialism isn't socialism, and Communism isn't Communism. I'm pretty sure our Republic is no longer a republic. I suggest everyone do an internet search: "Convention of States."

DECEMBER 1, 2018
FACTS OR OPINIONS?

How should we value our history? Does history repeat itself? Can history teach us to make better decisions? Should we be grateful to our ancestors? Should we blame our failures on the past? All are up for debate. All answers are opinions. The reality is, there are no do-overs; there are no what-ifs; whatever happened, happened. Only our perceptions are different than the reality of our history.

Some smart person once said, I'm paraphrasing here, "Those who do not learn from history, are doomed to repeat the mistakes of the past." I'm not looking forward to doomsday.

Hey, do some of you remember American history from high school? I trusted Mrs. Ruth, and the American history book approved by the Texas Department of Education. It was published in the 1950's, and there were lots of facts. If you learned the facts, you made an A. It was OK to have an opinion about some of those facts, but it didn't help your grade.

Several years ago, I was watching a high school volleyball game, and one of the students let me take a look at her history book. By golly, the facts have changed. The much more recent edition approved by the Texas Department of Education had some new and different facts. It also had some opinions which are definitely up for debate. The land of the free and the home of the brave is not so special anymore.

What happened to my heroes? George Washington and Thomas Jefferson were still there. But I couldn't find Nathan Hale or Patrick Henry. No Davy Crockett or Sgt. York. No Audie Murphy or George Patton.

Not only are some of my heroes missing, but we have changed the intent of the framers of the Constitution. When the founders were determining how the states would be represented in Congress, a slave was to be counted as three-fifths of a whole person. We are now critical of the South for not counting a slave as a whole person. The facts were, the Southerners who were involved in the writing of the Constitution wanted slaves to be counted as whole persons. The Northerners didn't want them counted at all. The debate was about representation. The three-fifths clause was a simple compromise. It had nothing to do with racism.

The ownership of another person was wrong. The Congress worked hard to pass amendments 13, 14, and 15, guaranteeing freedom, citizenship, due process, and the vote. But, when the Supreme Court decided Brown versus Board of Education and Congress passed the Civil Rights Act and the Voting Rights Act, I thought we had finally achieved the needed progress.

OLD WHITE MAN

But now, after years of righting wrongs of the past, there seems to be more division than ever. Freedom of speech is in jeopardy. Political correctness has run amuck. The uncivil are calling for civility. The truth is nowhere to be found. The politicians play "Gotcha," 24-7. The media and the elite clap. We're in trouble. Somebody throw me a rope.

JUNE 16, 2018

SPOILS OF WAR

Halt! WHO GOES THERE? FRIEND OR FOE? You dare not say, "FOE." Earlier this week President Donald J. Trump and Supreme Leader Kim Jong-UN answered, "FRIEND." Why not? All previous negotiations, starting from the position of foes, have been scary, to say the least.

A bit of Korean history. For over a millennium the Asian peninsula had been unified; however, as surrounding countries gained power, Korea was always defending itself against China, Russia, Japan, and even France. Prior to the end of World War II, Japan had control. After the war, the winning powers, US, Britain, the Soviet Union, and China took part in a trusteeship for up to five years with the goal of independence.

WHOA! The Cold War began and guess who became foes. The Soviets tried to put their guys in, and the US tried to put their guys in. They couldn't agree so the peninsula was divided into the North and the South. The Foes couldn't get along, and war broke out in 1950. Three years later, with over 40,000 UN deaths, mostly from the US, a ceasefire was agreed to, with a demilitarized zone between North and South Korea.

You know the rest. The South evolved into a democracy with a free enterprise system. The North, under the influence of Communist China and the Soviet Union evolved into a military dictatorship. The three Kims have been the three Supreme Leaders of the North, with free elections held for government officials in the South. North Korea has an economy of $40 billion, while South Korea's is over $2 trillion, that's trillion with a "t."

After the Singapore meet and greet, perhaps Kim Jong UN will want to adopt some Western free enterprise ideas, and start mending the steady decline of its economy. We can only pray the North Korean leadership will discover the advantages so apparent with its hereditary brothers in the South. We certainly can't predict what will happen next week, but at least the US is finally being proactive in solving 70 years of war and failed negotiations.

APRIL 28, 2018
FRONTIERS

Which way is the "Frontier?" Is it still there? My text this evening is from Frederick Jackson Turner, a noted historian who lived over a hundred years ago. He viewed American history as a moving frontier, first presenting itself on the shores of Plymouth, Mass. and Jamestown, Va. As Europeans made their way to North America, they encountered a wild and unknown frontier. Four hundred years later, the evolving idea of The United States of America is fast approaching warp speed.

As settlers, colonials, Indian fighters, northerners, and southerners moved across the land, built towns, fought for independence, and finally crossed the Mississippi, there was always a frontier; an edge where safety stopped, and danger began. Historian Turner believed it was the development of the west that best identified American Democracy. Out west, a man could find real equality. Courageous people took chances, claimed land, prospected for gold and silver, and many, not all, turned their life into the American Dream. There was plenty of violence and back breaking work. But, along with it, if you survived, a family had a chance to build a new and prosperous life, a real dream that could only be imagined in the not too distant past.

Is this dream still thriving? I think not. Somehow we got our dreams and our frontiers mixed up. I'm not sure when things began to go awry. Historian Turner believed it was sometime around 1890. Professor Turner believed the frontier stopped at the Pacific Ocean, and we were there.

As Americans, we have tried to repair the damage we inflicted as we crossed frontiers. We believe in the equality preached by Martin Luther King, and we have worked to undo the wrongs we heaped upon native Americans. It is time to figure out if the American Dream is still possible. It is time to find out if we can still negotiate the new frontiers of our American democracy courageously, fairly, and honestly.

We approach many frontiers today, none of which is easily defined with borders. Three important frontiers come to mind as I think about our future. One is space. We have begun to tinker with the great Universe. Star Wars may be a fantasy to many, but to me it is the future. Another, is found in the depths of our oceans. While amazed at some of the research available to the layman, the possibilities for discovery seem infinite. Finally, there is the human brain, perhaps the most complex frontier of all creation.

Perhaps, we can dream of one more American frontier. Is World Peace another frontier, or is it something else altogether?

HOLIDAYS

DECEMBER 23, 2017,
NO ASSEMBLY REQUIRED

Christmas traditions are special. The decorations, the glitter, the smells and tastes of cakes and cookies, the Christmas Tree, the lights and ornaments, the music, and many more customs are observed and celebrated this time of year, here in Texas, and all over the world. It's a time to enjoy family and friends, watch the joy on children's faces, and maybe share a snow ball or two. It's a time to make happy memories lasting for a lifetime.

There are two traditions I have eliminated to shore up my Christmas joy. The first is the, "Fruitcake." This Middle Ages custom needs to go in the dustbin of Christmas history. If you are so unfortunate to receive one, here are my instructions. Cut the thick loaf into three inch cubed pieces. Then gather outside for a contest to see who can throw a piece of fruitcake the farthest. It's important for appropriate rules to be in play. We must be sure not to throw a piece in a neighbor's yard. It should be legal for a thrown piece to be used more than once. Also, molding one into a spheroid shape should be allowed. Accuracy as well as distance could be incorporated into the new, "Fruitcake

Games." All manner of competitions may be integrated into new Christmas traditions. I can envision the fruitcake being substituted for a football. We might have to eliminate the kickoff, and the forward toss may be more productive than the forward pass. Fumbles may be hard to call, and even harder to enforce. A mighty fruitcake spike after a touchdown could be entertaining for fruitcake fans and players alike, and also the signal to get another fruitcake into the game. I can hear my grandson, "Just get me the fruitcake!"

The second tradition needing to go the way of the fruitcake is relatively new. It's the Christmas Eve practice for fathers, with the support and patient advice of mothers, to assemble the backyard swing set. I learned early on, the presents brought by Santa Claus would be stamped, "NO ASSEMBLY REQUIRED." Here's a sample of what a 21st century father may be getting himself into. The A-Frame Metal Swing and Play Set features a clubhouse with a hardtop roof, 2 belt swings, a trapeze bar, a 9 foot wavy slide, propeller swing, climbing wall, cargo net, activity board, a ship's wheel with binoculars, and plenty of activities to keep your kids and friends entertained in healthy play and muscle development. The play set comes with detailed instructions, a list of 13 needed tools, multiple bags of screws, washers, wing nuts, sets of bolts of various lengths, and an abundant supply of plastic caps. Two adults are required for assembly. You know you're in trouble when one of the tools is a, "Heavy rubber mallet." To maintain the spirit of the season, I suggest all young parents to ask the vendor the cost of store assembly and delivery. If that option isn't available, engage a civil engineer with an energetic elf, and pay time and a half for their consultation, skill, and labor. I promise you, you'll wish you had about 5 a.m. on Christmas morning.

Here's wishing everyone a very Merry Christmas, a Santa Claus experience, a long nap, and a Happy and Prosperous New Year. Maybe your football team will be invited to the Fruitcake Bowl next year.

DECEMBER 16, 2017
TINY TIM

Tis the season to be jolly, fa la la! All week long I have thought about many subjects that would be appropriate for this time so close to Christmas. I have reached the conclusion everything considered has been so overwhelming, the task would be a failure.

Knowing an honest effort at posting something of interest will only lead me down a rabbit hole, I have chosen to try my best to wish the world a very merry Christmas. Down here in South Texas, we are thankful for so much. First, being an American citizen is a blessing. Second, knowing I was born in the great state of Texas is a bigger blessing. Third, I have been visited by Santa Claus every year of my life.

Wow! A merry Christmas for the whole world. There are so many all around this world of 7 billion folks. My simple prayer is for all of us to be proud of who we are, and understand that everyone is our neighbor and needs to be just as proud as we South Texans are. To live on this amazing planet is special. As a child I always knew Santa

OLD WHITE MAN

Claus was circling the world, and he was coming to visit our home, the night before Christmas. I wish everyone in the world could have a Santa Claus experience.

My mind drifts to Tiny Tim, "God bless us everyone!"

MAY 27, 2017,

DECORATION DAY

Memorial Day is a special, but somber, holiday. It reminds us of the many men and women who have given their all, for all of us. I feel selfish when I remember some of my classmates who fought in Viet Nam. During that conflict, I was a young naval officer, and spent all of my active duty inside the Beltway, developing intelligence systems, at a 9 to 5 job, wearing a coat and tie. Our C.O. called inspection once a month; just to see if we still could wear the uniform of the day.

I am both humbled, and somewhat prideful by Memorial Day. This sacred day of mourning had its beginning by the Confederacy, shortly after the Civil War. The Union quickly followed with, "Decoration Day," as fifteen thousand soldiers' graves, in Arlington National Cemetery, were decorated with flowers.

My favorite American poet has always been Henry Wadsworth Longfellow, who penned, "The Midnight Ride of Paul Revere." He is not as well remembered for, "Decoration Day," honoring the fallen, both North and South, who gave their all, for all of us. With a bit of literary license, here is one of the last stanzas of Longfellow's poem:

> All is repose and peace,
> Untrampled lies the sod;
> The shouts of battle cease,
> It is the Truce of God!

The Truce of God is needed today. Truce is Peace, and it is needed each and every day. President Reagan understood our world needed, "Peace Through Strength." Unfortunately, the nature of mankind has never allowed us to find real peace, except through strength. On Memorial Day we need to pray for all who have given their lives so our lives are free. And, as lovers of freedom, let us all pray for Peace.

APRIL 15, 2017

EASTER FAMILY PICNIC

Today, I was fortunate to witness a big piece of the American Dream. It took place in West Nueces County, Texas, on the banks of Banquete Creek, under the bending branches, hanging with moss, spread out from a grand, old, thick trunked Live Oak tree. The occasion was the 75th annual West Family Picnic. There were 90 in attendance. The oldest are in their 80's, and the youngest is a smiling, seventh month old, young son of Texas.

My introduction to this annual event was 30 years ago. It was a few months before I married into this big clan, and we have attended every year since. Being outdoors on a bright, sunny, Spring day is always special, and today was exceptional. My wife's grandparents started this annual get together. They had eight children, who grew up, got married, and had a passel of children. Then, they all grew up, mothers, fathers, aunts, uncles, and now, grandparents, great aunts and uncles, and a few great, grandparents.

After everyone gathers, we spread all the delicious food on table after table. One of the older cousins calls us together, we join hands, and he gives us a grateful blessing. Then we sing a couple of old familiar Christian hymns. Eating a great meal with so many family members becomes a celebration. Some of the dishes have become annual favorites. My sweet wife bakes the same tasty apricot pies, once made by her Aunt Bea. I want to tell her they are just as good, but then I don't like to fib.

After we've shared the wonderful fare, the games begin. There are a number of professional horseshoe players, several expert baseball coaches and players, and some of us who just like to tell stories. All of this leads up to the event of the day. The egg toss is the serious competition. Watching is almost as much fun as competing. I focused on a three year old, partnered up with his grandfather. They didn't win, but were a formidable team.

It's always a bit sad when the party breaks up. There are lots of hugs, and a few tears. Some of the clan have to drive more than a day to get back home. We all look forward to the next Saturday before Easter Sunday, and another time to build more memories; memories we'll treasure as we witness the real American Dream.

DECEMBER 22, 2018

SCROOGE AND TINY TIM

The big question: Can Christmas bring change in a world gone astray? "A Christmas Carol," by Charles Dickens may give us light at the end of a tunnel. The time was 1843. The place was London, England. Working conditions were unbearable. Even young children were working in the factories. Think cold, dirty, dangerous, and dreary.

"A Christmas Carol," is a well-known story of economic greed versus the spirit of generosity. The celebration of the birth of Jesus Christ was enhanced significantly by Queen Victoria during the 1800's. She served over fifty years as Great Britain's monarch, and did much to influence the times, supportive of improving the plight of the working class. Although she had no vote, her opinions, feelings, and advice were taken seriously by the ruling class.

Enter Charles Dickens, the most beloved English author of the times. His short novel, written just before the Christmas of 1843, was an instant success. Economic greed was portrayed by Ebenezer Scrooge, who gains a spirit of generosity. The story is still possibly the second most popular Christmas story of all time, following behind the story told in the Gospel of Luke.

OLD WHITE MAN

"A Christmas Carol," still survives into the 21st Century, and has been adapted for films, plays, and recordings, numbering in the hundreds. In one of my favorites, George C. Scott plays Scrooge, and does it with excellence.

The night before Christmas, Ebenezer Scrooge had four very vivid dreams, the first with his deceased partner Marley, who was just as miserly as he, and then followed by the ghosts of Christmas past, the present, and the future. The next morning he was a changed man. Dickens' words were, "No space of regret can make amends for one life's opportunity missed!"

His bookkeeper, Bob Cratchit, had a happy family, even if enduring hard economic times. His youngest son, Tiny Tim, reminds us of a child, in the 21st century, living in St. Jude's hospital. Although small, sickly, and anemic, he had a beautiful heart. The ghost of Christmas in the future showed Scrooge witnessing the death of Tiny Tim.

The story reaches a climax on Christmas morning when Scrooge wakes up a changed man, reborn in the image of Christmas generosity. A grand Christmas dinner is shared with the Cratchit family, Scrooge gives Cratchit a raise, and Tiny Tim says, "God bless us, every one."

So, is, "A Christmas Carol," appropriate for today? I think so. I think we are getting tired of, "The Grinch." I've had enough of Christmas comedy. I believe we need to focus more on the sincerity of the real Christmas story. Yes, it's a time of joy and celebration...joy in the coming of a Savior, and celebration of the birth of Baby Jesus.

RUDOLPH AND THE DRUMMER BOY

Yep. We have lost our way. Christmas is drawing nigh, and we have failed; we have lost our ability to use logic, reason, and meaning. Political correctness has come out swinging against the music which accompanies the celebration of Jesus' birth, the joy of giving, the enjoyment of friends and family, and the season of merriment.

Christmas caroling may be in serious danger. The political speech police are ready to ban, "Rudolph, the Red-Nosed Reindeer." It seems the song encourages the young antlered reindeer to bully poor little Rudolph. They make fun of his bright, shiny red nose, and don't let him play reindeer games. Even Rudolph's dad is worried about his son's scarlet proboscis. Everyone knows who the big honcho is up at the North Pole. You guessed it; Santa Claus. On a foggy Christmas night, he called on young Rudolph to be the reindeer leader. And, according to all young children, he's been the leader ever since.

Next year, will probably be the end of the song, as well as the special Christmas movie enjoyed by children all over the world. Politically correct, current day kindergarten teachers will worry about Santa being an old white male. Next on the endangered list of songs will be, "God Rest Ye Merry Gentlemen." When the song includes, "Don ye gay apparel," you can guess someone will say the song was written by a deplorable homophobe. The song gained popularity in eighteenth century England, back when, "Gay," had a completely different meaning, distinct from the accepted definition found in today's Oxford English Dictionary.

There are numerous other Christmas songs in jeopardy. Here are just a few: "I Saw Mommy Kissing Santa Claus," "Blame it on the Mistletoe," "Baby, It's Cold Outside," and "Good Christian Men, Rejoice."

Then there's, "The Twelve Days of Christmas." I won't be surprised if PETA comes out against all bird hunters. How about, "White Christmas?" I'm surprised it's still plays on radio stations. I won't be bothered if we get rid of. "Grandma Got Run Over by a Reindeer." I certainly agree we shouldn't, "Give a license to a fat man who drives a sleigh and plays with elves."

Unfortunately, the thought police will give little praise to the special message of Christmas, brought to all of us with beautiful, timeless music. Handel's, "Messiah," written and composed in 1741, based on scripture, mainly taken from the gospel of Luke, combines a special vocal and powerful symphonic score, and is performed annually by hundreds of musical groups. Several Christmas hymns are favorites of all of us. "Silent Night," written 200 years old, has a visual sweetness to both words and music. "The Little Drummer Boy," written in 1941 is a more recent Christmas special, with a beautiful sentiment of giving and awe of the Christ child.

Is this the season to be jolly? You bet it is. It is also a very special season, one of unconditional love, unbelievable joy, and an amazing gift of grace. Enjoy it, be grateful, experience it, and also, be ever mindful of the Christmas needs of others. I believe Santa knows who has been naughty, including those politically correct folks. I'm sure they will find lumps of coal, ashes and switches on Christmas morning.

Here are some timeless words, without political meaning: "Christ was born in the first century, yet He belongs to all centuries; He was born a Jew, yet He belongs to all races; He was born in Bethlehem, yet He belongs to all countries." A quote by George W. Truett

MARCH 31, 2018
GOOD FRIDAY

Last night I attended my first Tenebrae service. Yes, I know, Tenebrae is one of those 50 cent words I just added to my vocabulary. The word comes from the Latin, a term for darkness, and became the name of a Good Friday service, that expresses the last words of Christ as He died on the Cross. The tradition began during the Middle Ages and continues in many Christian Churches today.

The service I attended was in the Grace United Methodist Church in Corpus Christi. It was a staged drama written by Ronald D. Vaughan, and the cast were not professionals, but were a very talented bunch. The drama presented several messages, taking us back over two thousand years ago, to hear in context the life of Christ, how we are a forgiven people, and God's commandment for us to love each other.

I've been thinking about living in the world today, and if we have learned anything during the past two thousand years. Yes, I think we have. Considering basic human rights and basic human needs, we have come a long way. What's troubling is our inability to wage a very successful war against the evils in our world.

Now! What's really troubling are our future prospects based on the thinking of Steven Hawking, purported to have been the smartest mind ever. Before he died he didn't tell us the importance of love and forgiveness. No, he wrote that as humankind continued to evolve, our survival instincts are evil, and we would eventually kill each other off. How depressing!

I have made an easy choice. I've decided to do my best to never watch, listen, or read anything about Steven Hawking. I do forgive him, and I wish him lots of love. Based on where he is now, he really needs it.

MARCH 17, 2018
SAINTS AND CELTICS

Today we celebrate St. Patrick's Day. Every year on March 17, all the fun loving, parade watching, party going, green beer drinking folks celebrate the feast day of Ireland's Patron Saint. His Grace, Bishop Patrick was born in England, but was kidnapped by some Irish raiders, and taken to Ireland as a teenager. He was worked like a slave, but with a strong heart and his faith in Christ, he escaped after six years in captivity. He experienced an answered prayer telling him to return to Ireland as a Christian Missionary.

He made his way back to Ireland several years later, after he had completed extensive studies for the Catholic Priesthood in France. Upon his return to the Emerald Isle, he converted many who had practiced paganism, including the worship of the Sun and the Moon as Gods. There are two traditions, continuing today, crediting St. Patrick for his teaching Christianity in Ireland. One is the Celtic Cross, a Christian Cross, with a circle intersecting each of its four points. This was Patrick's way of including the circular pattern of the sun and the moon, merged together with the Christian Cross. Celtic Crosses have increased in popularity over the years. In our protestant Methodist church, we have a beautiful Celtic Cross in a courtyard, admired by all. The other tradition is the three leafed shamrock. St. Patrick used this green clover as an image to teach the Trinity to his converts. If you are near a St. Patrick celebration today, you will see the shamrock on numerous signs, banners, and articles of clothing.

The myth of chasing all the snakes out of Ireland is false. Not to say he couldn't have accomplished this, but there weren't any snakes in Ireland in the first place. I guess it is comforting for Irish folks to know the serpent devil can't survive in their homeland. If you grew up in South Texas, and you want to go where there aren't any snakes, pick an island close to one of the earth's poles. I may make an inquiry to New Zealand.

The city of Boston, Massachusetts, has always had a strong Irish population. Irish immigration to America came with significant discrimination. Their Anglophile brothers looked down on them as a lower class. But, over time, the Irish have overcome the difficulties of their past, and are now represented in every kind of endeavor in the USA. Notre Dame University may have a French name; however, it's the Fighting Irish. The most successful professional basketball team of all time are the Boston Celtics, with a record number of championships. They are real winners, wearing their popular green and white uniforms, adorned with a lucky shamrock.

OLD WHITE MAN

Here's an Irish blessing for you on this 2018 St. Patrick's Day:

> May the road rise up to meet you,
> May the wind be always at your back,
> May the sun shine warm upon your face,
> The rains fall soft upon your fields,
> And until we meet again,
> May God hold you in the palm of his hand!

FEBRUARY 10, 2018

A BIT OF THE BARD

Okay guys, what's next Wednesday? That's right, it's Valentine's Day. Comes every year like clockwork on February 14. This particular day is critical for significant others to do whatever may fit each other's fancy. If breakfast in bed, candy, and roses, plus a dinner date won't do the trick, then I can't help you.

This day, named for St. Valentine, got its start in the third century when Emperor Claudius II ruled the Roman Empire. The story goes, a priest named Valentinus was doing his best to persuade the folks a good marriage was what everyone needed. This angered the Emperor as he was losing his warriors to pretty young Roman maidens. So, as Emperors were somewhat prone to do, Claudius martyred Valentinus. The frustrated emperor was much more interested in Holy Wars than Holy Matrimony. After the cupid priest was killed by the Emperor, Valentinus became a saint, thus February 14th became the feast day of St. Valentine.

Over the next 1800 years, St. Valentine's day became a very important romantic holiday. A bit of English Lit.

is needed here. Shakespeare used the day in several of his plays, for example in Hamlet, Ophelia is talking to no one in particular when she utters the following:

> "Tomorrow is St. Valentine's Day,
> All in the morning betime, and I a maid at your window,
> To be your Valentine.
> Then up he rose and donned his clothes and dupped the
> chamber door; let in the maid that out a maid,
> Never departed more."

I may be interpreting this a bit, but I think there's a possibility young Hamlet took advantage of the young and pretty Ophelia.

I always had a bit of difficulty with Shakespeare, but I have significant respect for the English bard and playwright. In my English Literature classes, as I remember, Cliff Notes made more sense for me than the originally written comedies and tragedies.

In conclusion, Valentine's Day was the reason for the rhyme,

> "Roses are red, violets are purple,
> Both are sweet, like maple surple."
> Pretty is as pretty duzz,
> Next to you, I get a buzz!"

MAY 11, 2019
MOM! COME QUICK!

Where would we all be without our mothers? Easy question; we wouldn't. Milton Berle is quoted as saying, "That evolution thing is failing since a mother has only two hands." Tomorrow is the second Sunday in May, and the day we honor the wonderful gift of Motherhood.

A little history; the Greeks and the Romans were the first to celebrate mothers as Goddesses, and each had a spring celebration to honor the goodness of Motherhood. Abigail Adams, the wife of our second President and mother to our sixth President, should also receive some celebrity as a special mother, who gave birth to six children, and fought against slavery even before it became an issue. Many of her letters to her husband, a leader of the American Revolution prior to becoming President, reflected a significant influence on his policies as a founding member of our country.

In 1872, Julia Ward Howe, who wrote the, "Battle Hymn of the Republic," lobbied for a day to celebrate Motherhood. It was to be on June 2, but it didn't come to pass. Ms. Howe was also an activist for the women's right to vote. A few years later Anna Jarvis, another activist for women's rights, was able to get the second Sunday of May as an official, "Mother's Day." Her life ended sadly. She honored her own mother, but she never married and was not a mother herself. She became very angry because Mother's Day was becoming commercialized. This year, approximately $25 billion will be spent honoring our mothers. When Ms. Jarvis was fighting for a special day for mothers, a congressman was quoted as saying, "A special day for mothers is puerile; every day is Mother's day." It seems every day we read about the special accomplishments of Motherhood.

Motherhood is priceless, but salary.com, writes the economic value of a stay at home mom is over $125 thousand a year; quite a hefty sum. When money is mentioned, debate enters. Is it really that much, or is it actually a lot more? Not in the mood for debate today, I would like to quote a Ms. Eluka Moore, who had this to say. "Motherhood is truly a remarkable gift, and a privilege I hold very close to my heart. To me, being a mother means to be fearless, to be a positive role model, to be a continuous cheerleader for every milestone my children will experience, to demonstrate the unconditional love that has no end and to cherish the countless memories that are truly priceless."

The gift of life is a miracle. We all need to be grateful for our mothers. They brought us into this world. They gave us the love and care that only a mother can give. Celebrate them, remember them, and bless them!

APRIL 20, 2019
EASTER EVE

Ohh…..The games people play. Today is Holy Saturday, the day before Easter. This week is filled with waiting. Waiting for the celebration of our Lord, Jesus Christ. While we wait, it's a good time to play some games to pass the time away.

I don't remember my first Easter Egg Hunt. What a great game. In D.C., the Trumps have invited any deplorables in town to bring their friends and neighbors to the annual Easter Egg Roll on the South Lawn of the White House. This tradition was begun about 150 years ago, and has grown to be a big event where no one uses political correctness when rolling hard boiled eggs with spoons down the slopes of the President's back yard. Many years ago some of the older children snuck into the White House kitchen and stole some spoons to be used to roll their eggs. Congressman Nadler subpoenaed the Justice Department for some spoons and eggs, but all he got were some cascarones which were unacceptable for rolling. This year the Egg Roll will be on Monday, April 22. One lucky youngster will find the Mueller Egg. It should be easy to find, since it will have a lot of egg on its face. Some of the eggs will begin to smell, and the Secret Service will have to find them and throw them away. They will be easy to find since they will smell like Schiff.

Meanwhile, most of the deep state people will be playing, "Pin the Tail on the Donkey." I remember being blindfolded, and spun around until someone handed me a paper tail, and headed me to the donkey pinned on the wall. I never won, since I wouldn't try and peek through the blindfold. There were always a couple of future politicians who were able to cheat, readjust their blindfold, see the donkey and find his a##. They would argue about who won while the rest of us kids were eating cake and ice cream.

The Deep State Game is a bit different. They used to divide themselves by party. You were a Democrat or a Republican. For the last 20 years or so, they have lost their ability to determine their own political party. They don't know the difference between a Jackass or an Elephant, so they have all joined a relatively new political party, "The Benjamins." Their symbol is the $, and when they play games, there is a ton of money involved. They play for big stakes, and since they all cheat, they don't use their own money. Us deplorables send them billions every year, but they continue to raise the bets. Someday soon, they will run out of other people's money, and they will have to move to Venezuela.

The most recent game in D.C. is the 420 Festival in RFK Park. It will be held today, and you have to have a government I.D. to attend. The goal is to create as much marijuana smoke as the deep state can handle. I've heard Congresswoman Cortez will be in attendance and present an award for the most natural strain of Weed, which releases smoke without a carbon footprint.

Another new game will be celebrated in towns along the Southern Border. A big piñata will be the target. It will be made in the image and likeness of President Trump, wearing a blue suit and a red tie. Whoever busts the piñata may be disappointed when no candy falls out, but the adults will be excited as green cards scatter everywhere.

Well, it's time to head for the giant live oak tree, on the banks of Banquete Creek. It's the Annual West Family Easter Picnic. The oldest in attendance weren't even born when the first one was held. Last year there were over 75 of us, some in-laws, a few outlaws, and many beautiful and handsome descendants of a wonderful South Texas Family.

We'll be playing some real games like baseball and horseshoes. There will be keen competition, but no cheating or money will be involved.

Happy Easter to all!!!

POLITICS

OCT 21, 2017,
LAW VERSUS TRUTH

QUESTION!!! DOES THE COUNTRY NEED MORE POLITICIANS OR MORE LAWYERS? Yes, it's a trick question. Volumes have been written about the doctors of jurisprudence wallowing in the quagmires of the legal system. Also, we have been reminded by reasoned historians, and lately by realistic populists, about the indigenous swamps encompassing the many ponds along the mighty Potomac.

It's time for a fresh EPA to target the wetlands of D.C. Our constitutional environment needs protection. How 'bout an EIS giving us cause to condemn all the reeking invasions of two legged, long armed squatters which are destroying the honored and monumental vestiges of our storied past. I like what P.J. O'Rourke wrote, "Even I realized that money was to politicians what the eucalyptus tree is to the koala bear: food, water, shelter, and something to crap on."

Doing a bit of light research, I arrived at a website, 'tentmaker.com," which displayed a graph detailing the number of lawyers per population size. The USA has three times as many as Britain, and forty times as many as Japan. What's up with that? Will Rogers honestly said, "lawyers can make crime pay." As the number of laws increase, so do the number of legal regulations and interpretations, thus the need for more practicing members of the bar. I can see our founding fathers up in heaven, telling each other, "I told you so."

Discarding the sarcasm, I believe we are in a very real world of, "HURT." I have a hard time finding truth and goodness. Injecting politics into everything has been so divisive. The word, "hate," was not used frequently in my earlier years. Today, it is such an invective, it has replaced many common profanities. In the year of our Lord, 2017, Corpus Christi, Texas, United States of America, it is time for, "LOVE."

SEP 30, 2017,
WHO'S YOUR HERO?

BORN IN THE USA, BOORRN IN THE USA, was an awakening to the misdeeds of the Viet Nam War. I was in my 20's, and the war was on the other side of the world. But I was very much born in the USA, during a more patriotic time, the early years of World War II. Everyone was proud to be an American. My heroes were two pictures of my uncle and my father, both doing their part in Europe, defeating Hitler, destroying the Third Reich. I naively believed all my fellow citizens were proud Americans. As a young student, a veteran, a corporate employee, and an educator, I was happy with the system. I believed people we elected to represent us, at every level of government, were by oath of office, required to serve the people. Naively, I was glad to elect all the politicians, who would naturally take their lead from the founding documents of our country. On election days, I exercised my right and my civic duty, and voted for the best candidate. Man, Ohhhhhh Man, I repeat myself. I was the definition of naivete.

I'm a Senior and am truly blessed. I'm also afraid, afraid for the USA, afraid for those who will follow me.

My hopes and prayers are for a resurgent America, an idea that embraces my children and grandchildren and all who want to live free. The last several elections, my votes have been cast for the least of evils. Our representatives do not represent the people. Maybe it has always been this way. Perhaps, America has never been the land of the free and home of the brave. What a depressing thought.

Our rights are God given. We are truly endowed by the Creator to have life, liberty, and the pursuit of happiness. We have free will, to make our own choices; to know, with God's help, we can leave this world a better place. This ain't gonna happen if we allow our rights to be taken away. My God, the local school district is making my old junior high school dump our mascot, "Rebel," to who knows what.

America has never been a perfect country. It is not utopia. No nation in the history of the world has been close to perfect. And some would have us all alike, in one world of (social?) justice? To think this hodge podge of 187 nations could come together under one world order is idiocy. These mundane thoughts haunt me. I see all the greatness that could be, but am blinded by the hypocrisy that is. Friends, we are being hoodwinked. The concept of social justice has been twisted to mean racism. The many definitions of racism lead me to know real racism is just unfairness. America was supposed to play fair. Have we reached the point of no-return? A news announcer told his listeners, the increase in natural disasters needs to be addressed. I was reminded of an old TV commercial ending with, "Mother Nature doesn't like unfair play."

I want votes to count. I want my country back. I want good neighborhoods. Most of us were taught to love our neighbors. Please raise your hand if you love your neighbor.

SEP 16, 2017,

WHERE THE GRASS IS GREENER

"Give me your tired, your poor, your huddled masses yearning to breathe free." These words have been taught to school children for over a hundred years. They were written by Emma Lazarus, and part of a sonnet, "The New Colossus," which can be found on a visit to the Statue of Liberty. If you include this icon on your bucket list, you can read the entire sonnet inscribed on the base of the statue.

Our country, right or wrong, is a nation of immigrants, as we are reminded frequently by some who want to open our borders to all comers. It's a noble idea, but our history tells we have not always embraced the immigrant. There have been many periods when we have encouraged newcomers, and quite a few when we turned them away. Yes, my friends, there have been many periods when we have opposed immigration.

The first people who migrated to America came across a land bridge connecting Siberia to Alaska. They came for survival. As the Americas' population grew, people have come for all kinds of reasons. The most recent wave of immigrants flows over the southern border of the United States. I believe this desire is something akin to the grass is always greener in my neighbor's pasture.

While researching the arguments for and against immigration over our southern border, I came across an organization which broached the subject with cross purposes. I googled a few of their academic panelists who appeared at one of their annual conferences. "Progressives for Immigration Reform," doesn't have a clue where their members stand concerning our nation's current discussion on immigration. The members do agree on conservation, so it seemed appropriate to consider the effects of immigration on our environment.

Quoting from their literature, "The National Environmental Protection Act of 1969 requires any federal program, policy, or project that might entail potentially significant environmental impacts undergo an Environmental Impact Statement (EIS)." It turns out that the EIS identifies many humans living in these United States will fall under the endangered species laws. The completed study by the Progressives for Immigration Reform includes the need to limit the number of humans coming across our borders to 250,000 per year. This is a 1,000,000 reduction in the current annual rate. If we don't adopt this reduction we will all starve by 2100. There won't be enough farmland to feed the people.

I'm suspicious of all environmental studies. Basically,

they're political in nature. However, when a progressive organization puts out literature warning us of future immigration, one wonders what the hell is going on? I'm hopeful my great grandchildren will find a place with open arms, seeking new settlers, like our country was once upon a time, "Taking our tired, our poor, our huddled masses, yearning to breathe free."

SEP 2, 2017,
THE 535

Here's my Saturday evening post: "Never underestimate the power of stupid people in large groups," George Carlin. I think the better quote may be, "Never underestimate the stupidity of powerful people in large groups." One only needs to consider the 535 elected members of our country's Congress. This group of ignoramuses (or is that ignorami?) has done less for more and more for less than any representative body in the history of mankind. Is "mankind," an OK politically correct term, as I want its meaning to be inclusive.

One realm of idiocy is the numerous spending bills that somehow make it through the legislative process. Many of these are horrible wastes of taxpayers' money. One of my favorite elected officials in the retired Oklahoma Senator Tom Coburn. Unlike many of his associates in the Congress, Senator Coburn considered his position one of trust and accountability. When he took his oath to the Constitution, he did so with humility and sincerity. Try googling, "Tom Coburn Wastebook," and you will source many entries about the $billions in wasteful spending on boondoggles and horse hockey. Coburn's annual "Wastebook," shines the light of day on our profligate D.C. Democracy.

Of more interest was his ability to cross the aisle and find common ground, ways for the people's real business to be done. Unfortunately for us, meaningful legislation continues to be absent. One would think the extremely low numbers for Congress would get their attention; however, failure after failure continues to be the outcome. I must cry out: "The Swamp Is Undrainable!"

DECEMBER 8, 2018
COURAGE OR POWER

My subject this evening is Ben Sasse, the Junior Senator from Nebraska. Is he a Man of the Heartland, from, "Flyover Country," or a tragic Conservative Elitist? College President Ben Sasse, a Republican elected in 2014 to battle Big Government Obama and the dems, was opposed to the nomination of Donald Trump. He is now in, "Limbo," as he works hard to support much of Trump's agenda, but does not voice support of Trump, the man.

"Them: Why We Hate Each Other, and How to Heal," published in October 2018, and written by Mr. Sasse is a predictable piece of non-fiction reflective of a Midwestern Academic. Sasse's personal history is exemplary. He graduated as valedictorian, from Fremont High School in Nebraska. Then, he may have made a left turn as he went to Harvard as a wrestler, and became an academic, getting his BA in 1994. He continued his studies, earning three masters' degrees from other institutions, and received his doctorate in history from Yale.

In 2009, he returned full time to his hometown in Nebraska, and served five years as President of Midland

University. Under his tutelage, the University made a significant, positive turn around, and is now a sought out private University, both academically and athletically. Originally, a Lutheran College, the school exemplifies the Protestant work ethic, and Dr. Sasse was a natural. He loves his midwestern ancestry, his family, and his Christian religion. When he took his oath to the Constitution, he was seriously motivated to work toward a return to the America he believed was blessed, and had the values so honored by the Bill of Rights.

In, "Them," he writes of his valid concern of the decline of our American culture. Our families are in jeopardy, our workplaces are tainted, and our neighborhoods are no longer safe. Face it, we didn't choose sides, we were influenced by others. Sasse gives an example of how your enemy in high school, becomes your friend when you meet again at summer camp. He differentiates Civics from Politics. Politics is the use of power. It is difficult to leverage political power with only a devotion to our constitution. In fact, I suggest it is impossible in our political arena. Lately, political power is being leveraged with hate.

He writes we must return to our roots. Not only personally, but in our communities and in our country. Civics is who we are, and we have forgotten our lessons of country and its rule of law. Politics is no longer the art of compromise but a battle for survival. I'm reminded of a quote from a movie; I don't remember the title. "There are no sides, there are no Republicans or Democrats. There are only haves and have nots."

For the Senator to succeed in his efforts to return to our roots he must become a fighter. As a man of faith, he must put on his armor and do battle. I believe he is conflicted. He doesn't want to put his reputation in jeopardy. He may not like the crassness, and the bluster of our Commander in Chief. But he better pray for acceptance, courage, and wisdom; acceptance of President Trump, courage to fight for a return to his American heritage, and wisdom to know when to pick his fights, and when to support his Commander in Chief.

CONSTITUTIONAL RELATIVISM

Can you remember forty years ago? I recall a Rotary Club meeting, and politics invaded my lunch. A friend commented, "Low morals and high taxes lead to the downfall of great countries." Are we there yet? What are America's morals? Are morals relative? Are we taxed too much? Are taxes used for the common good?

Consider the state of the U.S.A., right now, November 3, 2018, 3 days before a national election. Down here in South Texas, the lower environs of flyover country, do the elected and appointed elites inside the D.C. Beltway hear us? Maybe, but I think their listening skills need significant improvement.

This past week, I pulled out my copy of Robert Bork's, "Slouching Towards Gomorrah." Published back in 1996. There are two terms that have stuck with me, and I wanted to polish up on their use. They are radical egalitarianism, and radical individualism. Take away, "Radical," and they both are appropriate for democratic republics. Basically, we're talking about equality and individual freedom. Those two are right there in the preamble to our Constitution. America was built on equality of opportunity and rugged individualism. Now, it is equality of, "Outcomes," and individual freedoms get reduced regularly. I read the other day, someone called 911 from the drive thru at a McDonald's because the service was slow. You think I made that up, don't you.

Consider morals. Are they universal? Most philosophers disagree on this subject; however, when you consider behavior within a group, or a society, morals must be universal for the people to have success. The universality of morals was discovered with a bit of internet research and finding a Dr. Oliver Curry of Oxford University. His idea is, morals are universal when they promote cooperation. He lists seven moral values for success, 1) Love your family, 2) Help your group, 3) Return favors, 4) Be brave, 5) Defer to authority, 6) Be fair, and 7) Respect others' property. Unfortunately, our America has devolved into a myriad of politically correct, multicultural, economic, political, environmental, gender, and media driven dystopias, and we are unable to tell second base from a burnt biscuit. Our values are 180 degrees from being cooperative.

Do you really want me to consider the subject of high taxes? I didn't think so. It's something everybody agrees on, but nobody will do anything about. It's right there with so many issues we aren't able to solve cooperatively. Someone once said, "All politics are local." I think that guy is dead.

Perhaps we have let the cooperative value of deferring to authority, and allowed it to be far, far removed from our community's success. By the way, I'm wondering where God is as we struggle with so many national dilemmas. I will pray and fast on Monday with others as we seek an election outcome that is healing as opposed to hating.

AUGUST 18, 2018
YOUR WORD

Who in the hell said all politics is local? I'm not sure, but House Speaker Tip O'Neill had a book published in 1994, "All Politics is Local: And Other Rules of the Game." My grammar tells me politics can be either plural or singular, and since Tip writes of it as a game with rules, I suppose the title is grammatically correct. I know most of my older FB friends remember Speaker O'Neill, and some may agree with my opinion. I thought he was an irascible, hard drinking Irish Democrat from Boston, but a tough politician with a sharp tongue.

He and President Reagan had quite a few verbal exchanges, but both said they were friends after 6:00 pm. The first rule of the game, says Tip, "Some things about politics never change: Giving you word and keeping it is still the bedrock."

Both Ronnie and Tip are staring down from heaven, with disbelief, as they ponder the state of the game today. I may be naïve, but a person's word still carries some weight with me. Unfortunately, today, honest politicians are an endangered species. No longer bedrock, but sandy soil with only a few sprouts that usually don't last. There are probably a few sheriffs and JP's from sparsely populated counties in flyover country whose words still count for something.

Having the spunk, the courage, and the time to run for office, even locally, takes money, and the bigger the locale, the bigger the bucks. But, I digress, is or are all politics local? When it comes to the 1914 Nueces County Courthouse, the good intentions, and the frustrations of our local politicos, have finally hit that tar baby too many times. There's a great read by Dan Jenkins, "Stick a Fork in Me." Well, I think it may be time to stick a fork in the once, historical, and treasured Old Lady that has served as the entrance to our Sparkling City by the Sea. She has outlived the Memorial Coliseum and may outlive Corpus Christi's Harbor Bridge.

I'm thinking, I'll be gone when they start trying to save the 1977 Nueces County Courthouse, but there have been some rumblings we might need to start planning for the next one.

It's high time we award a contract to auction off bricks, pieces of beautiful terra cotta, and a few concrete sculptures. All the proceeds could be divided between the next, brave candidates who toss their hats in the ring to win a seat on the next county commissioners' court.

AUGUST 11, 2018
TALKING IS OVERRATED

I can't believe he said that! This week, I have heard or read some unbelievably stupid expressions using the English language. For starters, "Do you pronounce data, data or data?" Well that got me started. I found a bit of fun searching for all manner of quotes.

I really liked George W. Bush, but I wish he hadn't said, "Fool me once, shame on you. Fool me....you can't get fooled again." Somebody should have said, "George, that dog just won't hunt the second time." Of course, Secretary of Defense, Rumsfeld could have piped up, "There are known knowns, these are things we know we know. There are known unknowns. That is to say, there are things we know we don't know. But there are also unknown unknowns. These are things we don't know we don't know." I wonder if he stayed up too late the night before. Probably, practicing on how to tell the press he really didn't know much of anything. One thing I know, he didn't get a follow-up question.

There are also some really stupid quotes from some of our elected Democrats. I will never forget Nancy Pelosi, speaking of Obamacare, some 2,000+ pages long, "We have to pass the bill so that you can find out what is in it." Nancy is easy to pick on. How about this one. "Every month that we do not have an economic recovery package 500 million Americans lose their jobs." One of those fake news persons, probably followed up with, "How long before unemployment will really be in trouble?" Pelosi's most recent insertion of her foot occurred as she mused about California's outlaw of plastic straws. "The ban is important for gun control; it stops pea shooting and spit-balling which are gateway guns."

I don't think I've ever seen or heard of a gateway gun. One of our more talkative Democrats is Sheila Jackson Lee, who brilliantly stated, "I stand here as a freed slave. Freed 148 years ago by President Lincoln." I could really stretch this out with some Obama whoppers, but it's a rabbit hole too deep.

With an attempt to counter with a bit of wisdom, I'm going to add a couple of my favorites. "It's better to keep your mouth closed and let people think you are a fool than to open it and remove all doubt." Mark Twain. Here's my closer from Will Rogers, and truer words were never spoken. "The trouble with practical jokes is that very often they get elected."

JULY 14, 2018

FREEDOM OR CONTROL?

Do you remember your first vote for a President? My first was for Barry Goldwater in 1964. He lost, but his life was a lesson for all of us who love freedom, and believe in the miraculous nature of the human being. On Monday, July 9, Trump nominated Brett Kavanaugh as an Associate Justice of the Supreme Court. Many pundits, pols, and prognosticators have voiced their concerns about the direction the Court make take our legal system.

If this reignites the insight of our founding fathers and the importance of our constitution, the USA's ship of state may change its course and steer away from the Bermuda Triangle of moral relativism, big government, and corrupt bureaucracies.

The many news stories and editorials got me thinking about the trends of our nation during my lifetime, and they led me to reread, "The Conscience of a Conservative," published in 1960, by Senator Barry Goldwater of Arizona.

One of the initial concerns written by Goldwater was his own failure to voice the values and benefits of Conservatism. He equates the principles of Conservatism with the established truths of humanity and civilization such as the Golden Rule, the Ten Commandments, or Aristotle's Teaching of Ethics. He reminds us the Conservative approach is simply the attempt to apply the wisdom and experience, and the revealed truths of the past to the problems of today.

Almost sixty years ago, Goldwater gave us a step by step approach to political thinking. First, accurate understanding of the nature of man is required. Importantly, each man or woman is unique, blessed with the sacred possession of a soul, desiring both freedom and a meaning to life. Second, freedom is an illusion if man is dependent for his economic needs on the state. Third, the individual is responsible for his own development. He or she maintains their own dignity.

So, "The Conservative looks upon politics as the art of achieving the maximum freedom that is consistent with the maintenance of social order."

I believe this is what our founders were striving for as they wrote the Constitution. The framers knew the perils of power. They had experienced government by men who deprived the people of their freedom and dignity. The Constitution was their answer to giving each of us the best shot at a life of freedom and dignity.

Today, the greatest threat to us is any system, leading people to adopt increased powers of the state. The outcomes will slowly, but ultimately, be confiscation of personal property and increased taxes, furthering this confiscation. Goldwater uses a quote of Ben Franklin to stress the pitfalls, perils, and potholes which the Constitution does its best to avoid.

"What have you given us?" a woman asked Franklin toward the close of the Constitutional Convention. "A Republic," he said, "If you can keep it.!"

JULY 7, 2018

UPSET OR SUNSET

Dialectic Materialism....Now there's a term that can chase away readers. The term began as an argument for change due to the industrial revolution. It evolved, and revoluted (I just made that word up) into socialism and communism. You guys know something about those two, "Ism's." None of the people own anything. There is no private property. The state owns and directs everything. Why do I mention this potential drift in Western Civilization? I do so because of my concern with the continued activities of Barack Hussein Obama.

Have you heard of OFA? It stands for Organization for Action. The primary force behind this association of over a half a million U.S. citizens and illegals, is none other than our past first family, the OBAMA's. Where do they live and voice their distaste for our country's direction? How about a $9 million mansion, a couple of miles from the White House

Yes, the Obamas no longer control the Oval Office, but their work for, "Hope and Change," continues. Unlike other first families, they didn't ride into the sunset, but chose to continue with their unruly, disorganized friends and followers, and ride into the midst of fresh, newly organized communities.

Just exactly what does the Organization for Action do? It funds and supports community organizers. These are activists taught from Saul Alinsky's, "Rules for Radicals." Mr. Alinsky was a radical who taught, worked, and organized socialist movements during the middle of the 20th century. Two of his followers were Hillary Clinton and Barack Obama. Think of an activist group like Antifa. It's a weakly organized, community of demonstrators, frequently loud and violent, who are against whatever seems to be working for the common good.

Now, the Obamas will tell the activists of OFA they are organizing for the common good of the best ideas for America. What are the Obamas for? Here's a short litany: Abortion, Income Equality, Eliminate the 2nd Amendment, Open Borders, Big Government, Higher Taxes, Free Education from Pre-K to an Advanced Degree, Free Healthcare, Free Lunch; Uh Ohh... We forgot....there is no free lunch.

Just to get a glimpse of the Organization for Action, please look up, www.ofa.us. There's even a store where you can purchase a $10 T-Shirt for $30. Evidently, the OFA needs more than, "Righteous Anger." It needs money. Soros may run out. But not the Obamas. They're not about to sell their $9 million mansion, just down the street from the Oval Office.

NICKNAMES AND NAME CALLERS

What a week in the world of politics. Or, as some would say, "The Nightly News of the Nattering Namecalling Nabobs."

As a card carrying deplorable, born and raised in flyover country, I've been called a few unsavory names, and have thrown my share of epithets at friends and foes alike. I've always thought nicknames were terms of endearment, and were used in jest, wit, and kindly sarcasm. Willie Nelson proudly carries the nickname, "Booger Red." Unfortunately, our President has been called, "The Orange Hitler." I would suppose those who coined this nickname were, "Swamprats," or perhaps, "DemoRino Creatures from the Black Lagoon."

The, "Drive by media," the journalistic elites, and the pouting pundits have outdone themselves with numerous attempts to throw the catchiest negative nickname at our President. Here is a sampling of some monikers that have been bestowed on our Commander in Chief:

Donald Ducknuke, Donald Doom, Captain Chaos, The Fomentalist, Donnybaby, Trumpinator, Trumpenstein, Trumpletoes, Terrorist Sociopath, Two-bit Caesar, The

OLD WHITE MAN

Talking Yam, Captain Crunch, Hair Hitler, Adolph Twitler, and my favorite, The Twitter Terrorist.

Of course, the Donald likes to throw of few names of his own at many of his opponents. His timing is often spot on. When he called Ms. Clinton, "Crooked Hillary," it surely pierced the thin skinned ego of the, "Most qualified person in history to run for the Presidency."

Some may be concerned with the outlandish banter spouted about in the hallowed halls of our great bureaucracies, and inside the looping beltway surrounding our knee deep elected officials. But, methinks it's much ado about nothing, and it's high time we stopped our hypocritical, love affair with political correctness.

RIGHTS AND WRONGS

Eat your spinach. That's how I feel about Microsoft. I was happy with Windows 10, but my happiness is bubkiss. After clicking on, "remind me later," the Big Micro Mother in the Cloud said I had to install spinach. That's what I call my new operating system. And yes, they forced it down my palate right in the middle of my post. So far, I haven't realized any positives.

Now, I will try and revive my post. I started with:

Two, "WRONGS," don't make a, "RIGHT." But, can two rights make a wrong?

My two wrongs have occurred in South Africa. After a lengthy period of white oppression of black and colored people, Apartheid was finally stopped. A new constitution was written, and equality is supposedly the law of the land. Nelson Mandela and F.W. De Clerk were able to direct the change and stability, both needed for so many years. Each leader was awarded the Nobel Peace Prize.

Unfortunately, Mandela died in 2013, and the ANC, party in power, primarily native blacks, is unraveling. The current president of the party, and of the nation is a Mr.

Ramaphosa. He has significant hatred for all landowning farmers with white skin. He continues with vigor the confiscation of farms, without compensation, and thousands of white men, women, and children have been killed.

The ANC does not honor the constitution which guaranteed white farmers the ownership of their property. Definitely two, "WRONGS," with no, "RIGHTS." in sight.

Can two, "RIGHTS," make a wrong. My two rights are two attractive young ladies of color, Diamond and Silk. If you haven't seen them, look them up on YOUTUBE. They are quite an act, and support our RIGHT leaning populist president, TRUMP. They are smart and clever, and are opposed to the radical right as well as the radical left. They clearly see the establishment in the appropriate way. As most of my friends, and even some of my progressive acquaintances have seen the light, Diamond and Silk are not afraid to shine big floodlights on the deception of the political parties. These two, "RIGHTS," have been brought before Congressional Committees, and guess who tries to drag them down. Yes, the members of the Black Caucus have tried to get the best of them with phony questioning. My favorite example of a Black Racist is one Sheila Jackson Lee. I think these two, "RIGHTS," have exposed the wrongness of the Democratic Black Caucus. Sad...

BIG BUCKS FOR HIGH DOLLAR PORK

Waaaay toooo much noise lately. The news has been overwhelming; Pick any topic, and it is impossible to intelligently develop an appropriate opinion. So, after traveling down many rabbit holes, three weeks have passed me by without any focus. I'm doing my best to read good fiction, enjoy old Western movies, and watch sports. Even the sports channels have too much politics.

Unable to find any positives from the all things political, I have had some thoughts, having crept into my mind without invitation. George Bernard Shaw was a great playwright, but failed as an economics philosopher. Shaw was once quoted, "The government that robs Peter to pay Paul can always depend upon the support of Paul." Hard to disagree with that. He, of Pygmalion fame, was an active member of the Fabian Society which fit his Peter/Paul ideas into their musings. I remember learning about this snobbish English organization as a student at UT. The University would never present the subject today as it did over fifty years ago. The Fabians were socialist wolves in sheep's clothing. They proposed an orderly evolution toward a Marxist society. No revolution, just a slow direction of the great unwashed into a utilitarian society, without any disruptions. In case you haven't noticed, we're on our way.

As only an amateur political economist, I decided I would leave the Fabians, and take a look at how our welfare state has been wasting our taxpayer dollars. Do an internet search on, "Government waste." There are hundreds of sites to pick from, shedding light on the wasteful extremes we have achieved. For example, the feds spent $505,000 to promote specialty hair and beauty products for cats and dogs. I'm wondering if the Westminster Dog Show is unfairly benefitting at the expense of our beloved canine, "Odie," a proud Chaweenie, often mistaken for a Flop Eared Papillon.

I'm just getting started. Has climate change hit your weather radar lately? I just read where back in 2015, Obama paid his weather guys around $400,000 to tell him how we experience changes in our climate from time to time. I'm sure this was most important as he was advised where his Saturday and Sunday golf games were to be played. Can you believe he chose a course one Saturday, which immediately caused a cancellation of a club golf tournament. The tough guys in the big black SUV's instructed the golf course management to get all the tournament players to turn in their carts and find another venue.

Not to be outdone by Obama's climate change gurus,

NASA gave $250,000 to the University of Washington to study how rainfall effects the Red Crabs annual migration to and from Christmas Island. Researchers were hoping this study would help them better understand the potential consequences of climate change on this crab species. With a few more internet queries, I located Christmas Island in the Indian Ocean. Also, the Red Crab is a land crab species, possibly evolving with a red shell from the hot sun down south of India. As it turned out, the Red Crab has been attacked by Yellow Ants, which somehow were able to make the trip from Southeast Asia to Christmas Island. And here I thought NASA stood for National Aeronautics and Space Administration, and involved in space exploration. Just goes to show, if you're looking for some tax dollars don't give up easily.

Wasteful spending is an art. Most of it is included in discretionary spending, and it smells, thus the moniker, "Port Barrel Spending." I do need to give credit to two of my sources. First, retired Senator Tom Coburn, from Oklahoma, is a valid authority on government waste. Also, the Heritage Foundation has documented the topic thoroughly. I urge you to seek out Senator Coburn's annual wasteful spending books. I'd like to close with one of the wackiest items reported by the Senator. The National Institute of Health's Center for Alternative and Complementary Medicine spent $387,000 to study the effects of Swedish massages on rabbits. Believe me, you can't make this stuff up.

JANUARY 13, 2018

IN THE WEEDS

Can anyone tell me what is the "Deep State?" My limited research has led me to believe Deep States are ubiquitous and exist everywhere political subdivisions rule.

Here in the USA, Land of the Free and Home of the Brave, the Deep State is growing like kudzu. Those of you unfamiliar with this invasive plant, primarily found in the South, should worry, as it takes over about 150,000 acres per year. I'm not sure when our country's Deep State began to take root, but it has grown like kudzu for many years. At times it has been exposed by the nature of our healthy Constitution, but more often, its roots have spread out all over, disguising its weedy qualities with a pretty vine, yielding nothing but poisonous fruit. Yes, our Deep State is in serious need of Round Up.

By the way, did you know out national debt increases by $554,576 every minute?

We need to do some heavy pruning if God's country is going to thrive from sea to shining sea. I'm reminded of a song by Woody Guthrie, "This Land is Your Land." Woody grew up in Oklahoma and Texas; I'm pretty sure he knew his home was in flyover country. The talented, folk songwriter died in 1967. His lyrics may have been a bit more cynical if his song echoed the currents of today. I, for one, am struggling with the line, "This land was made for you and me."

Gosh dang it! We just incurred another $1 million in debt. It's hard to live in the moment when you're worried about the prospects of an American future for your grandkids.

The Deep State is not so fertile in flyover country, and isn't a threat to the kudzu. It's taken deep roots where the cherry blossoms flower, and the downtown city canyons get deeper and deeper. These are the places brought to light by the Tea Party, and Occupy Wall Street. The Tea Party rightly demonstrated in D.C for honest, transparent, and limited government, while Occupy Wall Street was just plain angry at the questionable injustices brought on the by those plying their trade amongst the cavernous canyons of Wall Street.

No, demonstrations don't get meaningful results. It's money and information, when combined with unscrupulous power that gets results. It's the unelected, entrenched bureaucrats in the Beltway who cowtow to the fortune 500 elitists, with their bought and paid for lobbyists. It's the gnarly, spoiled bankers of Wall Street who direct the flow of other people's money, and push their fast growing bamboo plants into the valleys of silicon. It would be a lot of fun and

OLD WHITE MAN

a real high to expose the Deep State. The problem is it's real deep, and most drownings take place in the deep end. Power and might, resulting from the sins of pride and greed, will probably always be with us, I'm very, very sorry, but the devil gave life to kudzu.

IS LADY JUSTICE UP FOR THE FIGHT?

Next week, I'll be posting with smoke signals. An hour ago, I had written to all of you, and as I was checking for grammatical errors, the big Facebook Spirit in the Sky came down and short circuited my work. I must be technophobic. I don't like these marvels from malevolent, silicon valley. I pretty much limit my use to a laptop at home and an iPhone 6 when I'm mobile.

So, next week I'm crossing the Nueces River flood plain, and find myself a good place to build a fire, and send my thoughts by carbon filled smoke. You know, two if by day, and one if by night. I wonder what AOC would do if she caught a Northeastern Mohawk cooking out on a campfire. I think wood burns cleaner than coal...probably O.K. since Native Americans are being persuaded to join the victimhood.

Back to the subject of my post:

ARISTOTLE: "At his best, man is the noblest of all animals; separated from law and justice, he is the worst,"

How's that law and justice working out for us these

days? It is much too simple to say, "The Law are rules of conduct, backed by state enforced penalties for violating such rules. Justice is giving each person what they deserve."

I could write all night about the injustices careening up and down Pennsylvania Avenue. Judges read the same laws, and come up with different outcomes. Interpreting the law is akin to saying, "The law is what I say it is!"

I don't know how a lawyer can even read the lawbooks. No one can read recent legislation passed by Congress. Ms. Pelosi already told us that. The Affordable Care Act, now there's an oxymoron, is over 2000 pages. An expert on the whole law probably gets six or seven hundred an hour just to tell Nancy what's in it.

Even down here in Texas, the law seems to grow without very good root structure. If you're rich, drive drunk, kill some people you'll get probation. If you're poor, drive drunk, kill somebody you get life. I think Lady Justice is losing her blindfold, and her scale is getting too heavy. She's already tossed her sword. Next thing you know, people will start tearing down all the lady justice statues because she's a racist.

Another concern I have is, why are all the Congressional staffers writing legislation? I don't recall one House or Senate staffer being on the ballot. Due to the number of TV screens filming gotcha Congressional investigations, our elected guys just don't have time to work on the business of the people.

Now, there's a novel idea. Let's all get together and tell our elected officials to work on the business of the people. They would just roll their eyes, and wonder, who's that rube?

THE GRASS AND WEEDS OF GREEN PASTURES

Well, are we changing the stars and stripes to green? These coastal elites are up to no good. Most of my friends from Flyover Country are 100% in favor of taking care of our land, our water, and all of us are grateful for clean air.

Have you read the text of the New Green Deal Resolution? It is currently being debated in the halls of the two highest legislative bodies of our Constitutional Republic. I don't know whether to laugh or cry. Our Congress has an approval rating bouncing around 20% favorable. This has been the norm for several decades. When we consider the Kool Aid consumed by some of these yokels, I'm ready to spike it with hemlock.

I'm glad not to be a scientist proclaiming the end of the world. What a miserable life. However, as a believing Christian, "thy kingdom come, thy will be done."

The text of the NGD states, "The Green New Deal will create millions of good high-wage jobs and ensure prosperity for all people of the United States." Yes, we will build resiliency against climate-related disasters, we will promote justice by stopping the historic oppression of the many political identity groups who have proclaimed victimhood. When you read this 49 page piece of propaganda, you will want to compare it to some of Stalin's five year plans. Reminds me of Obama, "If you like your plan you can keep it." Stalin just said, "If you don't like our plan you can go to a gulag."

The best way to seek some honest reality of what is going on in this world is to watch a few old YouTube videos by George Carlin. I'm paraphrasing here, "Take care of the planet? We can't even take care of ourselves. The planet has been around for 3 to 4 billion years. It's doing just fine."

Rep. Ocasio-Cortez and Sen. Markey tell us the GND will guarantee everyone a job with a family-sustaining wage, with paid family and medical leave, paid vacations, excellent medical care, and retirement security to all.

If I may be so bold, I don't know anyone with such guarantees. Not to say there aren't some coastal elites, in the top 1%, with pretty good gigs. All this good stuff will be had by all if we just adopt the Green New Deal. Show me some of that ocean front property for pennies on the dollar.

Let me close this week's less than optimistic diatribe with some information and a statement about Science and Politics. If you want to waste an afternoon learning about the Intergovernmental Panel on Climate Change, just google it up and get, "Information," where our new young congressperson and our old Mass. Senator get their facts about the coming destruction of the planet. Also, "In politics it's a matter of votes. With science it's never a matter of votes."

MARCH 2, 2019

AND OUT OF THE BRONX CORNER

Let's play, "Find the adjectives!" Outrageous...Scurrilous... Barbaric..., no I don't think I've gotten there yet. Let's see, how about...Half-baked...Laughable...Moronic...We're getting close...maybe, Threatening...Vicious...Satanic. Well, I might need to discard Satanic. But, I think I found some. Yes, I've been trying to find appropriate adjectives for the Gentle Lady Democrat first term Congressional Representative from the state of New York, the honorable Alexandria Ocasio Cortez.

Ms. Cortez is quoted as saying, "Unemployment is low because some people are working two jobs, and some people are working 80 hours per week." Selecting from above, perhaps we could apply, "Laughable." "Moronic," may be too strong. At least she is aware unemployment is low.

Now, there's this quote, "Any 17 year old can go into a gun store and buy an assault rifle." Sorry, that's just, "Outrageous." Federal law states a 17 year old can't buy any weapon more powerful than a water pistol.

Now, this next quote is somewhat mathematically

confusing. I choose to call it Half-baked. "Forty percent of Americans make less than $20,000 per year. That's over 200 million workers." Our country's population is 330 million people. 200 is almost 60% of 330. Is she just loopy, or perhaps maybe basic arithmetic isn't her thing. Does she think we should all move to Brazil?

With these bona fides she has launched the movement, "The Green New Deal." We live in southern Flyover Country, Corpus Christi, Texas, the Sparkling City by the Sea. Ms. Cortez tells us if we don't eliminate air travel, any engines running on carbon based fuel, rebuild all structures so no carbon based electricity is required, then those of us living close to sea level will drown from the rise in sea levels. Please save me some of that cheap, ocean covered property.

James E. Hansen, a NASA scientist, testified in 1988, before the Senate Committee on Energy and Natural Resources. He told those good old boys he had a high degree of confidence the greenhouse effect would cause major warming over the entire planet. His estimate sounded somewhat conservative. Maybe 1 degree Celsius by 2018. Scientists have to admit, there has been a possible 1 or 2 tenths percent of 1 degree over this 30 year period. This amounts to typical swings up or down since temperatures have been recorded.

Hansen doubled down in 2007, claiming sea levels would rise over 23 feet in the next 100 years. Between 1900 and 2016, the average rise worldwide in sea levels has been 16-21 cm. That's about a maximum of 8 to 9 inches over 116 years. Ms. Cortez, I suggest you spend some time learning your facts. Your intelligence indicates your Boston University Degree is an embarrassment to the administration of such a fine institution of higher learning.

But, I welcome you to the arena of sharing your ideas and thoughts with the American Public. I'm afraid you will need some very thick skin. You could be on the receiving end of some nasty adjectives. However, I know you are a child of God, and you are loved. So, stand your ground. It will be fun to watch you take on Exxon/Mobil, General Motors, Caterpillar, the Utility industry, and all those fat cats flying their private jets. And I sure hope you didn't offend Mr. Bezos when you told him Amazon is not bringing those lousy under $200,000 jobs to New York.

JANUARY 26, 2019
FIELD DAY

"A tight ship is a happy ship." First words I learned in the Navy, over 50 years ago. On board, there's a place for everything, and everything is in its place.

Since leaving the Navy, I spent the next 50 years unlearning those words of wisdom. Have you looked in your closet lately? Out on the ocean, there are no garages, no storage rooms, shucks, there aren't even any walk-in closets. So, the simplicity of the naval vessel gives us a command for neatness, cleanliness, and order. Alas, I can't give you a reason for the 27 burnt orange shirts hanging in my own cluttered closet. I refuse to count the pairs of socks, the t-shirts, the pile of underwear, and the many pairs of shoes, some of which have not been worn in over 30 years.

Having giving up on simplicity, I have given over to weak attempts at clothes and closet management, allowing me enough room to walk in the walk-in closet, and shut the door behind me. Since retirement, I have had plenty of time to simplify my life. The biggest impediment to this end is the struggle with throwing things away. For example, you just don't know when 26 burnt orange shirts may be dirty, and I'll have to depend on the 27th. A significant amount of discernment and discipline would be needed to reduce the number down to 15, but think of the gain in space.

Government could learn a few things from the Navy. Our ship of state, once a sleek, shining, schooner, skimming over the waters, selecting a new captain every four years or so, has turned into a gigantic rust bucket, with a mutinous crew, filled with jealousy, and backstabbing behavior. Emerging from World War II, the Government and Military decided to continue business as usual, and not having learned from experience, set itself on a course to become another example of the Titanic, and having sideswiped enough icebergs, we have begun to sink. Our new destination is Davy Jones' Locker.

We chose to keep the Home of the Brave and the Land of the Free on a war footing with high taxes and big spending. We were warned by President Eisenhower to beware of the military industrial complex. We did not listen to to his advice. I believe in a strong defense; however, our military spending annually exceeds the next eight largest defense budgets in the world, combined.

Here's a telling example of the success of simple common sense and the failure of self- dealing lawmakers thinking complexity can hide ineptness. In 1933, the Congress passed the Glass-Steagall Act, and it was signed into law by FDR. The law wisely separated commercial banking from investment banking. The legislation was 37 pages long. In

OLD WHITE MAN

1999, the Congress repealed the Glass-Steagall Act. Many believe this greatly contributed to the financial crisis of 2008. So, in its thirst for complexity, and corrective action, the Dodd-Frank Act, all 849 pages was passed into law. It has been a disaster.

Like many other complex juggernauts bubbling up in the swamp, inside the beltway, the pages of legislation are weighing down our ship of state. We're sinking into the black waters of an infested swamp. There aren't enough storage buildings or closets to hoard all of the clutter of government. Whether we compare it to a sinking ship, a cluttered closet, or an overloaded storage building, our government has weighed itself down to the point where we can't find an inviting dry dock, a clean closet, or an orderly storage room. In the Navy, when everyone stops whatever they are doing or not doing and cleans up the ship, making sure everything is in the right place, it's called, "Field Day."

In our ship of state, a field day is out of the question. It's time for the deep state to drown in its own diseased juices. Davy Jones' Locker is ready for a final resting place for the USS Beltway.

STUPID IS AS STUPID DOES

"Sometimes I wonder whether the world is being run by smart people who are putting us on, or by imbeciles who really meant it." - Mark Twain

The big news story of the day is, "The Wall." Someone once said, "Fences make for good neighbors." I'm not so sure we need to build something as divisive as the Great Wall of China. However, I'm in complete agreement with the concept of, "A country without borders is not a country." If the globalists think we're ready for a borderless, Kum Bah Yah, world, they need to return to kindergarten.

I did a bit of research on Nancy Pelosi's California Estate, and Trump's Mar A Lago. Ms. SOTH lives in a 3-story enclave surrounded by a 12 foot concrete wall. Maybe it's stucco, but it looks very intimidating. Mr. POTUS, when not at the Whitehouse, spends most of his time at Mar-A-Lago. He doesn't have any walls or even fences, but he has deep water on two sides, and a sophisticated security system.

We have neighbors on each side of our home, divided only by unseen, but surveyed property lines. We like to say hello to each other, but if we need to talk we use the phone, or ring the doorbell.

No matter, all of us want to be safe in our homes. Texas is my home, and most of the good folks we know and love are fellow Texans. People from Louisiana, Arkansas, Oklahoma, and New Mexico are neighbors, except at certain football games. The people of Mexico and Canada are international neighbors, and we have always had respect for the rules required to cross our southern and northern borders, coming or going.

I don't believe the electoral college selected Trump because he was a great American, nor did his voters believe he had a great track record as an outstanding corporate leader, or a man of honesty and integrity. He does have a history of getting things done. No, I tend to agree with Tucker Carlson. The voters elected Trump because, "it was a throbbing middle finger in the face of America's ruling class." One of the glaring truths of our time is the complete failure of elected and appointed public servants to respond to the needs of the electorate. I don't know if it has always been this way. I seem to remember a popular falsehood, "I'm from the government and here to help you."

Statistics are frequently used improperly. There are two percentages which appear often, and I believe to be accurate. 80% of the electorate are for term limits, and less than 20% view our national Congress favorably. If you are not in agreement, I am wary of your political preferences. Before

I turned 21 and was awarded the vote, I would sometimes listen to Edward Murrow on the radio or TV. I wasn't really a news junkie at the time, but the parents often viewed or listened to his news reports. I was lucky to live when he was the most revered news reporter.

In 1958 he gave a speech to the national organization of all big wig news sources, the likes of executives from NBC, CBS, and ABC. His remarks were widely read, and spread all over the news. He warned his audience of the dangers where news reporting was headed. Concerning the direction of the broadcast networks and commentators, "an incompatible combination of show business, advertising, and news media will become nothing but wires and lights in a box." He spoke of other newscasters, "Your reporting may travel halfway around the world, but you're no wiser than when you were at the end of the bar."

Good border security is desirable! Shouting for a big wall paid for by Mexico is a reach. Calling a wall an immorality is stupidity. As these are considered, let us all be reminded of the following: "Politics is the art of looking for trouble, finding it everywhere, diagnosing it incorrectly, and applying the wrong remedies." - Groucho Marx

SPECIAL

MAY 6, 2017

LISTEN, LISTEN, LOVE, LOVE

KAIROS 28 in the Connally Unit, April 26-29, 2017, was a glorious event. In 1976, KAIROS Prison Ministry International (KPMI) held its first three day event in Raiford, Florida, in a state penitentiary. Today, the ministry serves 472 prisons and communities, in 10 different countries, with 3 million hours of volunteer service per year!

The ministry chose the name, "KAIROS," Greek for time, not in the chronological sense, but in the sense of God's time. We believe this is a special time for both offenders and volunteers as we get to spend approximately forty hours with each other.

Volunteers are supported by an outside team, praying for us and fixing special meals, lots of tasty cookies, and plenty of fruit, all taken into the unit. "A man's stomach is the way to his heart," is not our motto, but in reality, it's a big part of sharing ourselves with each other. We take, "Breaking bread together," to a new level. There are forty-two offenders who participate in a KAIROS, and there are usually thirty or more volunteers who come in from the outside.

The Connally Unit is a maximum security unit located just south of Kenedy, Texas. KAIROS began serving this unit in March of 2002. We bring the Christian way of life into the unit. We represent many Christian Faiths, but we keep our Church traditions out. We want to listen to these men, and let God work his special love for them.

We continue to go back into the unit to meet with these men, pray with them, sing with them, and share God's love for them. Many men, inside and out, who participated in our first KAIROS at Connally, over 15 years ago, are still involved with the ministry. During this time we have brought KAIROS to over a thousand inmates. From the Bible's gospel of Matthew, Chapter 25, verse 36, Jesus said to his followers, "I was in prison, and you visited Me." It has been a special blessing for us, to see these men grow in their walk with Jesus Christ.

TRUTH AND FREEDOM

After reading our local fish wrap this morning, I fired off a letter to the editor. In a few words, I gave them my honest opinion. They don't publish my letters anymore. Nobody reads the rag anyway. I wanted the editors, such as they are, to know how I take honor in being a deplorable. It's sad to know how difficult it is to find and read the published truth. Whenever I think of, "Ye shall know the truth and the truth shall set you free," I'm reminded of MLK. I always knew those famous words came well before MLK, as I read them many years ago, almost daily, as a student at the University of Texas. The words are written in stone for all to see on the front of the University Tower, built during the Depression. The words came from the mouth of Jesus, in the Gospel of John, over 2000 years ago. Yes, my face book friends, we can always find the truth. It's in our Bibles. How very blessed we are.

SEPTEMBER 29, 2018

PRISON BUSINESS

What doth it profit a man, if, he gains the whole world, but loses his soul? A tough question, no? Just returned from a prison ministry volunteer team meeting. In a month, our team will hear the steel doors clang shut as we meet 42 men who live behind the walls of the Connally Unit, a maximum security prison in the state of Texas.

KAIROS Prison Ministry International has nine employees and over 30,000 volunteers. Kairos is a Greek word for time, not clock time, but, "A very special time." Volunteers take God's love inside the prison. There are more volunteers working outside the walls, making delicious meals, fixing bowls of fresh fruit, and delivering dozens and dozens of baked cookies. We're old school, and really believe the way to a man's heart is through his stomach. During this special time, a 4 day program, we get to witness the way God's love fills hardened hearts with food that may last a lifetime. WOW!

In the last 30 years there has been a 500% increase in the U.S. prison population. America is 5% of the world's population, and houses 25% of its inmates. I'm one person, with just 1 vote, but I do have an opinion. I believe we lock up too many people. There are those who need to be punished, but many need treatment for non-violent mistakes. Many volunteers, look back on their own lives, and admit, "There, but for the grace of God go I."

There is no simple solution to prison reform. Millions of philanthropic dollars have been given, over the last several years, to try and figure out this enormous problem. Grants can be given until the cows come home, but if governments don't embrace the issue, little will be done. Down here in Texas the prison system is Big Bidness. I want it to be Good Bidness. Please vote; it's a privilege. Voting your conscience is good for your soul.

JUNE 23, 2018

THOMAS SOWELL

A stroke of genius is when you find an economist for the common man. I lucked out when I first read a publication by the recently retired, Dr. Thomas Sowell. Sowell is pronounced, "Soul." His columns have not achieved the celebrity of Charles Krauthammer, but his achievements are remarkably similar.

Born in black poverty, 1930, in North Carolina, he was sent to live with relatives in Harlem. He was an excellent student, but dropped out of high school for economic reasons. In 1948, he tried out for the Brooklyn Dodgers. He soon joined the Marine Corps, and served his country during the Korean War. Upon returning to the States, He received degrees from Harvard, Columbia, and a doctorate in economics from the University of Chicago.

For many years Dr. Sowell wrote a weekly column, appearing in many publications, both in the U.S. and abroad. Every several weeks, he would title his column, "Random Thoughts." I have selected several of these random, and timely entries, for inclusion here.

"After a famous naval victory in the War of 1812,

OLD WHITE MAN

Commodore Perry reported: 'We have met the enemy and they are ours.' After the Republican Congressional majority's repeated capitulations to the Democrats' minority, Congressional Republicans could say, 'We have met the enemy and we are theirs.'"

Here's a good one, "Some Americans will never appreciate America, until after they have helped destroy it, and have then begun to suffer the consequences."

And, how about, "With the global warming zealots predicting catastrophic consequences over the next century, I wonder if anyone has studied how accurate five-day weather forecasts turn out to be."

A lesson for students, "No one will really understand politics until they understand that politicians are not trying to solve our problems. They are trying to solve their own problems...of which getting elected and re-elected are number one and number two. Whatever is number three is far behind."

Here's a couple of random thoughts of my own. "Over 300,000 illegal immigrants are serving time in our prisons for felonies committed in our country. Where's the outrage?" Or, "Do the democrats, media, socialists, and intellectually elite really want to eliminate our southern border?"

I will close with one of Dr. Sowell's best random thoughts, "What do you call it when someone steals someone else's money secretly? Theft. What do you call it when someone takes someone else's money openly by force? Robbery. What do you call it when a politician takes someone else's money in taxes and gives it to someone who is more likely to vote for him? Social Justice."

Dr. Sowell continues as a Senior Fellow at the Hoover Institution at Stanford University. He will turn 88 this June 30, 2018.

JUNE 9, 2018
CHARLES KRAUTHAMMER

We will miss Charles Krauthammer. Yesterday he wrote his last Friday column. It was short. His doctors have told him he has just a few weeks to live. He has suffered from stomach cancer for many months, but had thought it was in remission. The most recent checkup showed the cancer had returned aggressively.

In 2013, Mr. Krauthammer published, "Things That Matter, Three Decades of Passion, Pastimes, and Politics." Included, are many of his thoughtful columns, penned with a brilliance very few writers will ever achieve. A critique of any of his writings would lead to a praiseworthy analysis of readable prose. No words would be wasted, and seriousness, laced with timely wit, took you to a place, where you could only say, "Gosh, I wish I had written that!"

While it is difficult to choose a favorite column, I would like to share some comments about one of his best, published Friday, July 2, 2004. It carried the title, "In Defense of the F- word." Most of his columns ran from around 600 to 750 words; however, with this subject he could have covered up the entire editorial section, and I would have wanted more.

You know you're in for a treat, reading his first words, "I am sure there is a special place in heaven reserved for those who have never used the F-word. I will never get near that place. Nor, apparently, will Dick Cheney." It seems the President Pro-Tem of the Senate took offense at some backhanded comments made by Senator Pat Leahy, regarding some Haliburton contracts in Iraq. Krauthammer reported, with some glee, how Cheney had been efficient in his use of the F-word as a verb.

Krauthammer wrote, "By all accounts, he (Cheney) employed the pungent verb form, in effect a suggestion as to how the good senator from Vermont might amuse himself." I'm sure all would enjoy reading this column again. Just google, "Charles Krauthammer." Just reading about his life is an interesting read. Yes, I will miss Dr. Charles Krauthammer. Fortunately, I have, "Things That Matter," and will treat myself to his writings whenever political wisdom is needed.

MAY 12, 2018
RICHARD LEBLEU

It's 12:00, Wednesday, May 9, 2018. We're at the Riviera, Texas Cemetery. We are alerted by a call from the dispatcher, "Trooper 3614...Trooper 3614...Trooper is 10-7, 10-42." We hear the codes for, "Trooper is off duty and has gone home." Texas Highway Patrol Officer, Richard LeBleu has gone home, taken by his Savior Jesus Christ. The ceremony was steeped with tradition by members of our state's finest law enforcement agency, and blessed by Pastor Vallilea Blair.

Earlier, we attended a memorial service, celebrating the life of Richard LeBleu in the Christian Life Center of the First United Methodist Church in Kingsville. The Center was packed. The inside perimeter of the big room was lined with uniformed DPS officers. Several Officers were in full dress, and stood watch over the entire service. Listening, singing, and celebrating Richard's life was a special experience.

Richard LeBleu, retired Department of Public Safety Officer, served with distinction for 30 years: his childhood dream as a Highway Patrol Officer. His last several years, he worked in the Commercial Vehicle Enforcement Service.

These officers ride herd on the big rigs, over the road truckers. The job is essential to the safety of Texas Highways, and in South Texas, the name, "LeBleu," commanded significant respect from the 18 wheeler operators.

Richard personified the Department's core values of integrity, excellence, accountability, and teamwork. These values overflowed in his faith, his love of family, and his many friendships. He had a big heart, and an unforgettable sense of humor. We will all miss him. I close with the Highway Patrol Officer's Prayer:

"Heavenly Father,

Each time I walk this long walk, I pray I might be prepared to meet my confrontations I may encounter, that I might never be the undue aggressor, never lose my tongue in anger and always put forth my best efforts for each task. And, if ever I am called on to face the ultimate trial of life and death, that I might be victorious in the name of all for which I stand. Amen."

SPORTS

JUNE 30, 2018
GOLF, NO POLITICS

Rocky Mountain Highhhhh...Colorado!

This will be brief as I just finished my duties as a volunteer for the Senior Open.

It's a real blessing being inside the ropes, here at the US Golf Association 39th Senior Open. Standing with my direction paddles on the 9th Tee, signaling where tee shots are launched, with the weather at 77 degrees, sunshine, and humidity at 20%. Colorado Springs, the Broadmoor East Course is the venue for this year's open, and it's special.

Everybody's favorite is Fred Couples, but Jerry Kelly's got the lead by one going into tomorrow's final round. These guys are good! All these players are over 50 years of age. Golf is truly a sport you can enjoy into your golden years. Golden is literal for the competitors this week. The winner will take away several hundred thousand in legal tender. Yep, they're playing in their golden years, playing for golden prizes. What a life!

The greatest thing about the last few days; nobody seemed to care or mention the daily noise coming out of the Beltway. Everybody just wants to talk about golf. I'm lovin' it.

OCT 7, 2017,

Texas fight, Texas fight, Yea Texas Fight!

Great game today. The Longhorns were tough. Always fun to walk away a winner.

HOOKEM!

JUN 3, 2017,

DON'T YELL AT THE UMPIRE

Lots of goings on this week, so this will be brief. At least, as it compares to some of my other billets. My text comes from, "The Tao of Willie." That would be one of my favorite philosophers of Central Texas, none other than Willie from the Nelson family.

I've been spending quite a bit of time trying to Let Go, and Let God. That sounds simple, but putting it into practice requires years of patience, acceptance, experience, and above all, wisdom. Willie says, "It's not a perfect world, and sometimes you just have to let your anger go." If you can manage to let your anger go, and let God, then you are living life in the right lane.

Recently my anger has attempted to get the better of me, and it's mostly directed at high school baseball umpires. I've worn corrective lenses most of my life, and I believe my eyesight is superior to any baseball umpire anywhere, anytime. I'm positive I can see if a ball passes over any part of the 17.5 inch wide home plate. Umpires have a way of varying the width of home plate with personal discrimination, which is clearly taking advantage of some batters over others.

Forty years ago, I coached little league for five years, and I was only thrown out of one game for questioning an umpire's call.

Sitting in field box seats at an Astro Game, at about the same age, I could yell at an umpire like all the other loud mouthed fans, and know I could keep my seat.

Today, as an aging Grandfather, I've had to learn to keep my mouth shut when attending one of my grandson's baseball games, and it has been a difficult learning experience. I know I need to let my anger go, and let God be in control.

Willie would rather have me get mad about the cost of health care, and be more concerned that illiteracy is too rampant.

Willie writes, "My general philosophy has been to never miss an opportunity to shut up," a bit of wisdom, I wish I'd learned as a child.

ZEBRA AND THE CLOCK

Are you a procrastinator? A website, tipsywriter.com informs that this personality characteristic has increased substantially over the past 30 years. My first reaction is this may be a direct correlation to the increase in fake news columns. I remember Charles Krauthammer's routine of putting out a weekly column. He allotted time for thinking, researching, outlining, and preparing a rough draft before he wrote his column, and then spent a bit of time editing until it was submitted, always on time. Of course there was the rare occasion Dr. Charles would inform his publisher he was taking a few days off, and would forego his once a week submission.

I don't have a publisher, and don't think Facebook would publish any of my stuff anyway. However, I have been posting fairly regularly over the past two years, and have several facebook friends who I consider to be loyal readers. I am humbled that anyone would enjoy my writing, and this has motivated me to try and post something each Saturday.

My honesty does not allow me to make an excuse for not getting to my weekly task yesterday. So, I am including procrastination as one of many personal, human flaws needing to be addressed. It would be foolish of me to think I could make any significant improvement to my "POW," difficulty, "Putting Off Writing," syndrome. So, I prefer to simply say, I watched the entire Texas vs. Texas Tech game last night. While I struggled in my recliner for most of the game, I was exhausted by the last 30 seconds when Texas scored to untie the game, eking out a win in a very evenly matched competition.

All football games seem to last so much longer than in the past. For a game with 60 minutes on the clock, the telecasts last over 4 hours more often than not. Lately I've been watching old western movies to occupy my time during all the long delays caused by commercials and the referees. All seven or eight zebras have to consult whenever a piece of yellow laundry hits the turf. They either don't know how to enforce the rules, or have developed severe, "POC, Putting Off Calls syndrome," including the plethora of, "The previous play is under review," interruptions. Last night was no exception as Apache Charles Bronson eliminated an eleven man, tainted posse, starring in, "Chato's Land." The movie started in the first quarter and was over by the end of the third. I missed a few clever, eliminations of corrupt western lawmen, but I can explain the entire plot if asked.

Lots of writers are overly optimistic about their writing ability to get the job done, and may have developed POW syndrome. I've always been more optimistic than the alternative; however, it is problematic when considering the glass half full or half empty. My engineer friends tell me the glass designer should have called for specs to be 50% smaller. Today, everyone seems to be drinking out of very large glasses which leads me to my next explanation of POW.

Being a drinker has also been a cause of procrastination. I can speak from experience; it is no fun writing when you are hung over. But, I have been clean and sober for almost 23 years, so that is not a source of my current POW. I know many have struggled with procrastination, but don't be self-critical. It is definitely not sinful, and is often overlooked by the person who is obsessively compulsive, who spends too much time worrying about when the game starts, and rarely gives a hoot who wins.

OCTOBER 6, 2018
PREAMBLE: WORDS TO LIVE BY

Today, the Cotton Bowl, in the middle of the Texas State Fair, a piece of hallowed ground, located in the Southern parts of Flyover Country, was a special place. The Texas Longhorns eked out a win over the Oklahoma Sooners. Hookem!

If you're my friend, you're probably from Flyover Country. Where did we get the moniker, Flyover Country? About 70 years ago, Lockheed built the majestic Constellation Airliner. It could easily fly from sea to shining sea, usually from New York to Los Angeles, and the Redeye, from Los Angeles back to New York. A passenger could look down on Flyover Country; the deserts, the Rocky Mountains, the Bread Basket, the Rust Belt, the Great Smokies, and enjoy a three point landing at Idlewild Airport in New York.

Some folks think of Flyover Country as the Heartland of America. The Heartland is not just geography. It's where the real bodies, minds, and spirits of our people build their lives. In 2016, I listened to Hillary tell me I wasn't living in the Southern Bread Basket of the Heartland, but I was in a "Basket of deplorables, a racist, sexist, homophobic, xenophobic, Islamophobic." I had to look up "Xenophobic." It means to be afraid of people from other countries. All of us trespassed into America from somewhere else. I guess her meaning was "We are all afraid of ourselves."

Evidently, I still have a lot to learn. I am an old white Texan by birth, by faith, and by God my father. And, oh my gosh, I'm male. Willie Nelson said he was glad when he learned when to shut up. In the recent Judiciary hearings, Senator Hirono told us old men to just shut up. That's a lesson I've had trouble learning, frequently having to insert my foot into my mouth. My parents, both born in Flyover Country, taught us conversations at the dinner table should be of general interest. That meant don't talk about religion or politics.

I'm jumping out on a limb here, but I want to believe Flyover Country is defined neither by religion nor politics. It should be defined by the Preamble to our Constitution. John Wayne said, "Words are what men live by." The Preamble includes some of those words, such as, "To form a more perfect union." It seems we are working hard to form the opposite. How about, "Establish Justice." Not social justice, not economic justice, but, "Justice." The Preamble uses, "Insure domestic Tranquility." I'm looking hard for domestic tranquility. The Preamble asks for the, "Blessings of Liberty." Freedom is a blessing, but it isn't free and it ain't insured. It must be earned, protected, and defended.

OLD WHITE MAN

As a boy, I was taught when I reached 21, I could exercise my own vote. It has always been important to cast my one vote. I can't remember a time when I felt anyone wanted to deny me this right and responsibility. The good folks volunteering at the polling precincts have always been friendly and gracious. I try and make a thoughtful choice. When someone makes another choice from mine, I still respect the voter. It's the person who doesn't vote who loses respect. I try to love the intellectually elite, the entertainment elite, the corporate elite, and the government elite. The elites seem to be at their best when they're in coastal areas. They don't like to spend much time in Flyover Country. I'm going to pray we all meet in the middle.

SEPTEMBER 15, 2018
SCOTLAND OR HEAVEN

"Methinks it is a silly game," said King James II of Scotland in 1457. He was speaking of the game of golf as he watched his soldiers hit balls around the sheep meadows outside of his castle. They were taking a break from practicing their archery skills, and the King believed it was a waste of their time, so, he banned the new sport.

The Royalty, however, kept the game going, and during the next century golf became popular not only in Scotland, but throughout the British Isles. Mary, Queen of Scots, took up the sport, and was so successful, she was able to beat all her male courtiers. She had her military cadets carry her clubs, thus the term, caddie. Queen Elizabeth, became jealous, so she made up a story about how Mary would cheat. There is one story, she moved her ball which was a violation of rule 10, "If a Ball be stopp'd by any person, horse, dog, bones, or anything else, the Ball so stopp'd must be play'd where it lies." Whatever the case, Elizabeth, being the more powerful Queen, had Mary's head chopped off. The rules of golf have continued to grow in complexity, and the penalties have become less severe.

OLD WHITE MAN

The young men of Scotland had such fun with their new game of skill and patience, they would not be denied. By the 18th century, golf had made the eastern coast of Scotland its permanent home. Its headquarters still exist today at the Royal and Ancient Golf Club, in St. Andrews, Scotland. The village is a few miles north of Edinburg, and the, "Old Course," is where golfs' greatest players have won the, "Open Championship," and the 12 month ownership of the silver Claret Jug, now a symbol of golf's greatness. This year, the winner, an Italian, named Frankie Molinari, got the trophy, along with $1.8 million. Back in the late 1800's, the first monetary prize was awarded, approximately $400 in current cash. Today, there are over 2,500 golf courses in the British Isles, which is the highest concentration of golf land use in any country in the world.

Over the years the game gained in popularity, and finally made its way to America. The Pilgrims and the Puritans were opposed to the game as it was seldom played without a few friendly wagers. During the late 1800's a number of British immigrants, with golfing skills, had arrived in America, and soon, golf took over the Eastern Seaboard. Americans, when they engage in a sport, become the most skilled, and by World War II, the United States was home to most of the greatest golfers of all time.

I started to write a few remarks about golf and politicians, but I regained my composure, and thought better of it. Mark Twain, not a politician, but a great wit, when asked his opinion of golf, said, "It's a good walk spoiled." It's always good to quote a Yogi-ism, "90 percent of putts that are short, don't go in." Here's one from Gary Player, "I owe a lot to golf. It's a debt I'll never be able to pay." On the nature of the game, Arnold Palmer said, "Golf takes more mental energy, more concentration, and more determination than any other sport ever invented." My favorite from Mr. Palmer, "When I was in college I thought about being a lawyer, but I wasn't smart enough, didn't like being indoors most of the time, and besides, I'm too nice a guy."

Some folks think golf is a sport for the rich, but I strongly disagree. Here are a few facts about Lee Trevino. He grew up in Garland, TX, with his single mother and grandparents. He never met his father. He started picking cotton at age 5, began caddying at age 8, and quit school to work at a driving range. After 4 years in the Marine Corps, he turned pro, and became one of our country's finest professional golfers. He was fun loving, and loved the game. Once, in a playoff with Jack Nicklaus for the U.S. Open Championship, he tossed a rubber snake at his opponent on the first tee. Everyone got a laugh, including Nicklaus. Trevino went on to win the playoff by three strokes.

From September 28th to the 30th, the Biennial Ryder Cup Championship will be played in France. This will be the first time ever in France, and only the second in Continental Europe. The teams are twelve of the best golfers from the States paired against twelve of the best from Europe. It will be fun to watch, and very different from most golf championships. It's Europe against the Red, White, and Blue, Home of the Brave. The golf will be amazing and the matches will be tense. Watch it if you get a chance. As opposed to the NFL, it will not be unpatriotic to be patriotic.

My father was an avid golfer, and his several trips to play golf in Scotland were some of his favorite times. When he was on his death bed, we talked about what a full life he had lived. Somehow, the subject of going to heaven got into the conversation. He looked up at me with his twinkling eyes, and whispered, "I'd much rather go to Scotland."

SEPTEMBER 8, 2018
SPOILED WINNER

My Texas Longhorns got corralled last week. Having to play inside the Washington D.C. Beltway must have messed with our flyover country team. It's hard to come up with any other excuse, except maybe the jinx of the Longhorn TV Network. I swear, since the University took ESPN to the cleaners, and angered the rest of the BIG 12, it's been pretty slim pickins for the football program. Since the LHN's existence, we've had two coaches fired, one winning season, and two yards rushing in the Texas Bowl, three years ago. Yep, it's pretty difficult to look forward to Saturdays this fall.

When it comes to football, I've been spoiled. My high school won the Texas Championship the year after I graduated. The Longhorns, under Darrell Royal, won their first National Championship in 1963, the fall after my graduation, and I've been a Cowboy fan since Tom Landry coached them in their inaugural season.

I must give credit to the Sewanee University of the South's vaunted football past. My parents wouldn't let me attend UT my freshman year. They believed, with good evidence, that I would drink too much, and not make my grades. So, I got to go to an all men's school, an Episcopal College on a mountain in Tennessee, in a dry county. We had a winning football team, I made my grades, and got to transfer to Texas, and watch Darrell Royal win some of the greatest games ever played. But before I leave Tennessee I need to write about the Sewanee Iron Men of 1899. They were 12-0, and won the Southern Intercollegiate Athletic Conference. The team only had 21 players, and they traveled by train to play opponents. H.M. Suter was the coach, with no assistants.

This team was unbelievable. They played 5 road games in 6 days, and won 'em all, shutouts. They beat Texas, 12-0, A&M, 10-0, Tulane, 23-0, LSU, 34-0, and Ole Miss, 12-0. The team won 12 of 12, all shutouts but one. 322 points to 10. You may think I'm making this up, but google the, "Iron Men of 1899," and you'll be a believer.

Now, here I am, a happy senior citizen, without a football winner. My lesson for this week is patience. I've been an Astros fan since they were the Cot 45's, and played outdoors. Now, in 2018, after over 50 seasons, the Houston boys of summer are the defending World Series Champions. What really teaches patience is when you're used to having winners, and it seems to end. I'm not a fair weather fan, so I will continue to love the Longhorns, wear orange, and hope for the good old days. When you keep up that hope, you've got patience whipped.

APRIL 7, 2018
THE MASTERS

I missed my deadline yesterday. I tried to write something, but my subject was the Masters Golf Tournament, and I couldn't get anything good going because the tournament wasn't over until about an hour ago.

WOW!!! What a Masters! What a win for Patrick Reed! The young, 27 year-old has had a lot of success on the tour, but this is his first Major victory, and it was dramatic. He held the lead by three strokes at the start of the day, and it wasn't easy holding on to it. Every time he made a poor shot, he followed with a great putt, or a super approach shot.

Patrick, dubbed Captain America by some of his fans, was born in San Antonio, and his home course is the Woodlands, just north of Houston. He's a real Texan, but he chose to play his college golf at Augusta State in Georgia. He had a lot of local knowledge this week, and today he showed us how to navigate among the Georgia pines and Southern azaleas.

My Dad died thirty years ago, and I was fortunate to be with him when he watched his last Masters. His routine was to get to Augusta on Wednesday, watch the Par 3 tournament, watch Thursday, Friday, and Saturday, and then drive to Birmingham, and watch Sunday's round on TV. In 1988 the winner was Sandy Lyle from Scotland. He made an amazing shot on number 18 out of a fairway bunker to win by a stroke.

I don't remember what Sandy Lyles' winner's check was, but think it was around $100,000. Patrick Reed's payout today was $1,980,000. Not bad for four rounds of golf at the most beautiful golf venue in the world. I usually stay away from superlatives, but believe me, if you haven't witnessed the beauty of the Augusta National Golf Club, put it on your bucket list.

My bride and I met my Mom and Dad in Augusta to watch the 1988 tournament. She was impressed by the beauty of the place, and her not being a golfer, it was fun for me to tell her some of the quirks of the game. We were watching players hit into number 13 green, and I told her, "Wait till you see where the pin is tomorrow." She said, "Do you mean they move the hole?" I'll never let her live that one down.

For me, golf is the most difficult of all sports to master, and I believe the game teaches us a lot about life. Every shot you hit is different, and sometimes you are so lucky you let your pride get in the way. After a few good shots you start to think you know what you're doing, and then you miss a few, and it seems like God let the devil get in the way. Last month I was holding court about the difficulties of hitting a golf ball at rest, and an old baseball player said, "Try and hit a 100 mile an hour fastball." I had to eat a bit of crow.

Next year, Patrick Reed gets to determine the menu for the annual members' dinner before the tournament begins. I sure hope he picks one of the entrees to be Texas brisket. One thing for sure, nobody there will eat any crow.

MARCH 24, 2018
BAGGER VANCE, PHD

"Take a mulligan." Some of us hear the word, "Mulligan," and think of an Irish stew. Golfers know the term as a gift from another player, in a friendly game where nothing of any value is on the line. When you stand on the first tee, and you miss the first shot of the day, one of your playing partners may say, "Take a mulligan." That drive you just duck hooked into the trees won't count. You get to tee up another ball and see if you can find the fairway.

So, one of your friends gives you a mulligan. Getting to replay that first shot of the day may mean the difference in a good round and a bad one. You didn't earn that extra shot. In the game of golf there are no do overs. You can't find the word, "Mulligan," in the rules of golf.

In life, most of us need a few mulligans along the way. Second chances in life can mean the difference between success and failure. It' bigger than that. Second chances can be so significant, a person's life can be changed in such a meaningful way, it's like he or she was born again. Uh Oh, I bet you're thinking I'm gonna get religious on you.

No, but I think I may be heading toward a bit of,

"Spiritual Illumination." Knowing how much I love the game of golf, one of my grandsons gave me, "The Mulligan," for Christmas a few years ago. It's a great little book about golf and more importantly, a book about life. The book was written by Wally Armstrong, a retired professional golfer, who now teaches and writes about the game of golf, and Ken Blanchard, who identifies himself as the spiritual officer of the Ken Blanchard Companies, a global leader in workplace learning.

The book teaches us how a perspective on the game of golf can teach us how to succeed in the game of life. Getting the gift of a mulligan in golf is like getting a second chance in life. Second chances and mulligans are gifts. We didn't earn them, and they aren't deserved. They are true gifts, given by someone who cares.

In golf, the professionals have a caddy carrying their golf bag. The bag contains all the tools of their trade. It includes fourteen clubs, extra balls, gloves, an umbrella, and other foul weather gear. The caddy is much more than someone carrying a bag of clubs. He or she can be a coach, a consultant, an important friend, a teammate, and yes, often, a spiritual advisor. Google up, "Bagger Vance," a great movie starring Will Smith and Matt Damon. Watch the movie, and you will see how all of us need someone to help us as we play the game of life.

FEBRUARY 3, 2018
BUCKET LIST?

It's Brady, the old gunslinger, versus Foles, the overachieving veteran. It's the Patriots against the Eagles, sounds kind of political. Most individuals who desire to serve their country think of themselves as patriots. At least that's what I thought when I wore the country's uniform. Non-military service was patriotic also. I'm not sure about that anymore. Whatever? I'm not letting any memories get in the way of a good football game. Tomorrow, we should be entertained by two great professional football teams, who will duke it out for the National Football League Championship. It's SUPER BOWL SUNDAY!

The Philadelphia Eagles will do their best to upset the New England Patriots. We could also connect a bit of patriotism with the Eagles, as they chose their mascot to be the American Eagle. They picked the name since the Liberty Bell is in Philadelphia. Perhaps we Americans can get some patriotism by osmosis if we pull for a great game, may the best team win, and the loser fight a great fight. By the way, if the Eagles win, it may be an omen as they are no longer on the endangered list. If two teams from the

Northeast don't get your attention, it might help to know quarterback Foles got his start in Texas, at Austin Westlake High School.

Most of us begin the season wanting our favorite team to make it to the big dance. Unfortunately, the Dallas Cowboys have been in absentia for over 20 years. Our blue and silver America's team with Troy, Emmitt, and Michael have all hung up their cleats, and living in the fading sunshine as deserving members of the Pro Football Hall of Fame. How the ego driven owner Jerry Jones every bribed his way into the Hall of Fame as a contributor in 2017 is beyond me.

You may enjoy some Super Bowl Trivia; most food consumed on any day of the year except Thanksgiving. Some say more beer is consumed than any day, but I'm not sure about that. Lately, some women's groups have pushed for a crackdown on increased domestic violence with all those macho men drinking all that cold beer, but real research doesn't confirm it. The cost of a 30 second commercial is over $5 million, the result of record TV viewership.

If watching the Super Bowl is on your bucket list, I'd take it off. The average cost of a ticket this year is over $5,000, In addition, the work of travel, traffic, parking, maneuvering through rude people, finding your seat, and dealing with a fan in front of you who wants to stand for the whole game, you're pretty much exhausted by halftime. A comfortable couch seat in the den, a few steps from the fridge, and a wide screen HDTV looks better every year.

Over forty years ago, I attended Super Bowl VIII, at Rice Stadium in Houston. Miami and Larry Csonka beat the hapless Minnesota Vikings in front of a packed house. As I recall, my ticket was given to me, and the price on the stub was in the $20 range. The University of Texas Longhorn Band was the halftime entertainment. Watching the showband of the Southwest will beat Justine Timberlake exposing Janet Jackson's right breast every day of the week and twice on Super Bowl Sunday.

APRIL 13, 2019
FINDING TRUTH

Can anyone find the truth? Who lost it? Did America lose it? Is it gone forever? I've been searching everywhere, and I'm worried it may be gone. Are there any universal truths? Is there reality in our world?

I want to believe in reality. But lately, it seems everyone argues about what reality is. I've been watching the Masters Golf Tournament this week, and I'm 100% confident in the truth of a golf ball in flight. If there is truth in beauty, then I know I have found truth in Augusta, Georgia. If I could live behind the 13th green, and experience the flight of a golf ball on its way to land on the green and roll up to the flag for a tap in eagle, I know I will have found truth in beauty. The reality of an eagle made on number 13 is true reality. When the red three goes up on the big scoreboard, we have found truth. We have experienced reality. The joy of excellence is evident. The beauty of the Augusta National Golf Course is reality.

With golf, things are so much simpler. If only life could be lived on the golf course. Golfers play the hole as it is. When a good shot is made it is acknowledged by all who witnessed it. Professional golfers play for money. When someone wins, he wins. Golfers take the game as it is, and learn to live life as it is.

I'm a Christian, and I must confess I have violated the third commandment while playing the game of golf. Like life, golf often hits us with a degree of frustration that requires all your patience, and an ability to hold your blood pressure in check. If you have faith in your game, you will find enough enjoyment to bring you back for another great experience on the golf course.

While truth and reality are easily found on the golf course, they are difficult to locate as we search for them in other avenues of life. When we get trapped into following the noise of politics, I'm pretty sure truth, reality, and ethics are a thing of the past. There was a time, right here in the United States when people accepted each other as they were. We all knew everyone fell short when it came to living a life without sin. But, forgiveness is nowhere to be found. The truth of unconditional love is hard to find. There is no trust. Moral relativism is scary as hell. No one seems to want solutions.

Greed, anger, and evil are on the rise.

Technological complexity may be the planet's downfall. I'm content to know the truth of who is in control, and it ain't us. I'm willing to let go and let God. If I'm fortunate to arrive in heaven one day, I pray I will get to play golf. All the golf courses in heaven will be like Augusta National, and I'll get to tee it up with Ben Hogan, Arnold Palmer, and Slammin Sammy Snead. I won't even be nervous on the first tee, and when I pull out the big dog, I know God will help me hit long drives, right down the middle. When we get to the green, I'll be saying, "Arnie, it looks like you're away."

TRIVIAL PURSUIT

DEC 9, 2017,
ONLY THE ROCKS KNOW

A good friend suggested I write a piece on, "How to teach a rock to talk." Teaching a rock to do anything is a Herculean task. Rocks have a mind of their own. I'm reminded of a hunting buddy from long ago, asking an old cowboy why there were so many rocks in the Hill Country. His answer, with a touch of wisdom, "Why son, rocks are what hold the world together." If one attempts to write of the corporeal qualities of rocks, we can conjure up all kinds of examples. Spend a few days in Yellowstone Park, and you will witness the living, breathing, moving, growing, and entertaining evidence of what's happening just below the outer crust of our planet. Perhaps a more successful endeavor would be to ask the rocks how to teach the rest of us a thing or two.

Anthropologists, zoologists, biologists, geologists, ologistsadinfinitem would be lost without the fossil remains of all sorts of living, evolving history. Cave pictographs were painted on rock walls. Carvings on rocks, rock formations, and carved rock walls; all this evidence from the past has contributed immensely to current knowledge of the physical and biological sciences.

Perhaps the most talkative rocks have been diamonds and gold. Bankers are quick to tell us money talks, B.S. walks. Diamonds are rare, pristine, bright, and valuable. Their price rises geometrically based on size and brilliance. Several years ago, I remarked on the rather large diamond solitaire ring worn by the mother of a friend. Her response, "Thanks, Honey, I've always said there are two rocks in the world, Gibraltar and mine." How about those gold rocks? Definitely pricy nuggets. You can buy river rocks for as low as $.05 a pound, while river nuggets of gold sell for around $20,400 a pound. No wonder all those 49'ers headed to Sutter's Mill in California. I bet those 49'ers from San Francisco would quit kneeling if they were treated to a few valuable rocks. Or, better yet, maybe I could get the concession on small river rocks sold on game day, for fans to throw at the kneelers, getting their attention, and perhaps they would stand up and show a bit of respect for the Stars and Stripes. The price would be substantially greater than $.05 a pound.

Considering the forces of nature, and the hands and tools of builders and sculptors, we can hear the sounds and teachings from many types of rocks and many spectacular rock formations, I believe there is much to admire in the world of rocks. Standing on the edge of the Grand Canyon, taking in its awe and beauty, gazing at the rock layers of history, is possibly the greatest rock show ever. For sure, it's a lesson on our mortality. God wants us to believe and have faith in our immortality. If you google up the, "Churches of Lalibela," you will be introduced to one of the wonders of our world: eleven rock-hewn Ethiopian Christian Orthodox Churches. Each of the monuments to our Creator is chiseled out of the town's red volcanic rock hills. (Information courtesy of Wikipedia.) The last church to be completed, the Church of St. George, is shaped like a cross. It was completed over 700 years ago. The artisans who worked to create these amazing structures had tremendous faith, and surely earned their immortality.

FOOD FOR THE FUTURE

What do the Fountain of Youth and Phytoplankton have in common? Yeah, I know; who gives a rip? Most of my Facebook friends are more interested in life after retirement, and any new great panacea, stamped with FDA approval, or perhaps, the approval of the Panamanian authority for food safety, is good to go. I use Panama as a credible source of food safety and potential panaceas, as I know the water is safe to drink.

For those of you who remember Biology 101, phytoplankton is the largest source of food for the biggest, and most prolific eaters in the world. Long living, huge leviathans of the deep, and many species of fish live on a diet of phytoplankton. The actual food cell is too small to be seen by the naked eye, but if you're looking at satellite film taken hundreds of miles above the earth, you can see it in abundance in the world's oceans.

Perhaps you might want to google, "phytoplankton health supplement." Don't be fooled by the many hucksters singing the life giving properties of this superfood. Man has been searching for the fountain of youth for thousands of years, but if you dig down into the many health qualities of the hundreds of phytoplankton types, and also recognize the tremendous food supplies from our oceans, some very smart marine microbiologist may be on the verge of finding a real fountain of youth. This sounds a bit like quackery, but I feel I'm in a tight race for human spirituality, against artificial intelligence, so I'm in favor of cheap, good food as opposed to cheap, clean energy.

So, what about Ponce De Leon and his discovery of Florida, searching for the fountain of youth back in the 16th century? Historical facts don't support the travels of Admiral De Leon, but a Spanish conquistador, Admiral Menendez, did establish St. Augustine, Florida, the oldest European colony in America. He spent most of his time fighting with natives, and French Protestants, so the importance of finding magical waters seemed a poor use of his time. He was successful in building this historical community, and it still exists today. Florida's school for the blind is in St. Augustine, and claims Ray Charles, one of the most spiritually gifted humans ever. I know if Mr. Charles were alive today he would let artificial intelligence go the way of Ponce De Leon.

NOVEMBER 17, 2018
DON'T WORRY, BE SORRY

"What, me worry?" Many of you may remember Alfred E. Neuman from, "Mad Magazine." Surprisingly, Alfred gave us good advice. Does worrying ever yield dividends? I think not.

Unfortunately, even though I know worrying is not productive, the mind goes its own way toward those brain cells harboring the worry syndrome. "Live in the present," I say. Then you won't worry about something you can do nothing about.

Listening to the environmental philosophers leads to unnecessary worrying. In the late 60's, scientists, spending their lives worrying, warned us about global cooling. After learning air conditioning didn't boost global cooling, they began to worry about global warming. Now, the scientific elite lobby our Federal Government to spend billions trying to stop the damages made to Mother Earth by big, bad corporations, and also by the little bitty landowners.

These scientists were rewarded by the establishment of the EPA, the Environmental Protesting Agency, by President Tricky Dick Nixon. At first, the government passed the

OLD WHITE MAN

Clean Water Act and the Clean Air Act. After we cleaned up the water and the air, the agency had to find some new environmental problems or its budget would be in jeopardy.

The EPA started out with a budget of about $1 billion, and less than 5,000 employees. Hopefully, its annual spending of over $8 billion has peaked out. It is a sizable government agency overseeing the work of 15,000 bureaucrats. Some of the hundreds of topics with EPA oversight include asthma, bed bugs, bees, civil rights, methane, composting, fish, light bulbs, glyphosate, mosquitos, etc. I could go on for pages.

Today, environmentalism has become a religion. The intellectually elite have shouted the need to take care of the earth. This has become more important than taking care of our fellow man. The funding for these efforts often come from the titans of Wall Street and Silicon Valley. That would be New York City and the San Francisco areas. It is in those places and similar ones in large urban areas where we have forgotten to take care of each other. The homeless crisis is worse than any environmental problem facing our country. The streets of Manhattan and San Francisco are worse than the many natural disasters we face every year.

Yesterday is history, and tomorrow is a mystery. We need to live in the present. Worrying doesn't get anything solved. I'm sorry, but I worry everyday about those homeless folks. Worrying about them doesn't help, but I pray for them, and I know the Lord has not turned his back on them.

OCTOBER 13, 2018
NORTH PLATTE, NEBRASKA

Benjamin Franklin once said, "The mouth of a wise man is in his heart." Yes indeed, there's some wisdom! I think our national dialogue could use a big dose of Ben's wisdom.

Most of the national dialogue is heard, blurred, and slurred in our country's big cities. Think New York, D.C., Chicago, L.A., and San Francisco. There are lots of good folks from those gridlocked places, but lots of good folks have not moved to the congested urban areas. Out here in the Heartland, in Southern Flyover Country, most activities revolve around getting the kids to school, working to support a family, going to PTA meetings, and Friday night football games. But if you get lured into the fast lane of our nation's biggest metropolitan areas, you may end up on the dark side.

To experience the bona fide, real life of our fellow Americans you need to find a good town in flyover country. One of the hundreds of great American towns right in the middle of the contiguous forty-eight is North Platte, Nebraska.

If you travel across the country by bus, train, or auto, from New York to San Francisco, you will likely pass through

North Platte. It's right on IH 80. and North Platte is a high per capita town when it comes to comfy hotel rooms. Stop and spend the night. Get up and visit the Golden Spike Tower, and you can see for miles. You can also take an up close and personal look at Bailey Train Yard, the largest train yard in the country.

Yes, North Platte, Nebraska, is Flyover Country, in the crossroads of the USA. The unemployment rate is low, the people are real, and they're friendly. Citizens are honest, and community is important. It's the kind of place where you can breathe in fresh air, a place where people know and trust each other. Shucks, you might even want to add it to your bucket list.

POTHOLE HISTORY

Black holes, worm holes, sinkholes, and rabbit holes, all manner of holes. You've also got your post holes, water holes, and swimming holes. However, the hole causing the most angst, quickest anger, and maximum frustration is the worst hole of all, the dreaded, dangerous pothole. Maybe, if we hadn't developed asphalt, civilization could have avoided the pothole.

The first recorded use of asphalt for road material was in the deserts of ancient Persia. The Babylonian king, back in 750 B.C. decided to use some tar, mix it with some sand, and have his slaves lay down a nice road from his palace to the gates of the city. At the time there wasn't a written word for asphalt in the Sumerian language. Over time the word's origin was found in the Greek, and it was pronounced as-phal-tos.

Evidently, there was an over-abundance of tar, and the Persians started exporting the material to the Gulf Coast of Texas. This being prime flyover country, the Karankawa Indians were grateful for the tar, and using their Texas ingenuity, they used it to cover their bodies, protecting them from the burning sun.

Little did they know this substance would later be mixed with sand and gravel and become a most popular paving material. Today, one can drive all over the state of Texas on asphalt roads. Back in Persia, it's pretty much all desert and without much rain the asphalt roads would last for ages. Not so, here on the Gulf Coast. We are blessed with an annual average of over 30 inches of rain, and asphalt being porous, water and traffic tend to cause potholes.

This abundant rain, our shifting soil, and our heavy pick-up trucks have played havoc with our asphalt roads, We reside out in Northwest Corpus Christi, in a nice little area called River Forest. I'm not sure when the first asphalt streets were built, but my guess would be over a hundred years ago. A pioneer named Calvin Allen settled this area almost two hundred years ago, and he probably bought some prime asphalt from the Karankawas.

One of the streets I maneuver to get to the Interstate is Mountain Trail. The street is 1,050 feet long and about 20 feet wide, give or take a few feet. That measures over 20,000 square feet of asphalt, or perhaps I should report approximately 12-13,000 square feet of potholes. It might be more appropriate to report, "Patched potholes." I can't use the term, "fixed," or "repaired," as these patched places are frequently re-patched, or even re-re-patched. I've tried to count them a few times, when our flop eared papillon, Odie, and I go for a walk. My counts have not been consistent as it's hard to determine when parts of the street are the result of multiple potholes in the same place.

I've considered suggesting Mountain Trail for a Geology field trip to some of the local schools. The lesson would be figuring out the ages for the different patched potholes. Over time, the color of the asphalt fades, and one wonders if the pothole was there before the street. In keeping with our trade policy, maybe we could place a tariff on imported asphalt. Or, better yet, what with global warming and climate change our rainfall may be curtailed, and then there wouldn't be any water to seep down into the asphalt, thus eliminating our potholes altogether.

AUGUST 4, 2018

HOT DOG DAYS

Whew.! The Dog Days of Summer. How did we ever manage without air conditioning?

I was wondering where the phrase, "Dog Days of Summer," originated. I figured it must have come from somewhere south of the Mason Dixon Line. Was I surprised when I googled, and learned it came from the Greeks, around 750 B.C. This sheds a bright new light on global warming.

Quoting from Homer's, "Iliad,"

> "On summer nights, star of star's Orion's
> Dog they call it.
> Brightest of all, but an evil portent,
> Bringing heat and fevers to suffering humanity."

The Greek word for this brightest star of the night sky is Sirius, a point of the constellation of Canis Major, (Big Dog?). Sirius was named after a Greek goddess, and she carries the title, The Goddess of the Dog Star. The bright star makes its appearance in the summer sky, and was thought to be responsible for the oppressive summer heat.

Today, we must deal with the reality, or perhaps the politics of global warming. I prefer the term climate change. I must say the dog days of summer give me pause to consider the trend of global warming. Growing up in Corpus Christi, I don't remember the summer heat being quite so stifling.

The Greeks would have us believe global warming has been around for some time. If you research the subject today, it's only been about 25-30 years when the political and scientific communities have been overly concerned. Doing a bit of internet surfing you will find a myriad of graphs, opinions, scientific theories, global observations, and supposedly certified facts proving our coastal plains will be under water by 2030. I'm wondering why beachfront property keeps going up in price.

The climate scientists think their research and findings are so accurate in predicting rising temperatures and coastal flooding, you'd think we could get an accurate weather forecast for more than a day or so. I don't think those of us in flyover country make many decisions based on global warming. For example, I plan to walk our dog, Odie, this afternoon, and it's pretty hot outside. I suppose I could wait until dark, but we have our routine, and 30 minutes outside will do us both some good.

By the way, the movement of the heavens will navigate Sirius over the next 10,000 years so that it will make its appearance in the winter sky. Perhaps the earth will begin to cool again. I hope some of those climate scientists are still around to observe the expansion of valuable beachfront property.

JULY 28, 2018
AGING AND LEARNING

Many, many, many thanks for all my birthday wishes from so many friends. Your wishes came true. My 77th birthday was a keeper. A pair of 7's gets beat by two Aces, but I'll bet a few chips it'll be a winner. I'm starting my eighth year in my eighth decade, and I am truly blessed. One of my heroes, John Wayne said, "I do think we have a pretty wonderful country, and I thank God he chose me to live here." I've been thinking a lot about our wonderful country, and I've begun to wonder a bit about us, but I'll postpone those thoughts till when I'm a bit more pensive. Right now, I got that "Joy Thing" working better than middling.

While I'm in this good mood, I'll share a few of my ideas about how to age happily and wisely. First thing, make sure you stay in the game. My favorite game is golf. I'm not too old to play now and then, and I like to keep up with what's happening in the sport. I really enjoy watching the game's best players compete. This week the pros are playing the Canadian Open, and one of the leaders is Whee Kim from South Korea. His name and his size reminds me of Tiny Tim, but he can, "Drive for show and putt for dough."

OLD WHITE MAN

I don't know what your game is, but I do know we need to suit up every day. I always keep my clubs in the trunk of my car.

A second good plan for aging gracefully is knowing when to talk and when to shut up. Willie Nelson, another one of my heroes, taught me this bit of wisdom. After over 70 years of experiences on this earth you start thinking you know most of the answers. But most of the time just when we think we know the truth, something gets in the way. The Judge in the Divorce Court always knows there's his story and her story and the real story. Sometimes things need to be said. John Wayne, as Jake Cutter in, "The Comancheros," told us, "Words are what men live by....words they say and mean." I'm learning to think before I say something, which is pretty good advice for any age. Yep, lifelong learning is a necessity.

I've got a few more, but I hate to get too wordy, so I'll leave you with just one more idea about good aging. Stay in the Moment! . . . . Whew, there went one, but there's another coming right now. Enjoy it. Watching a good movie, reading a good book, working on your game, listening to a favorite song; those are filled with wonderful moments that you're just in. Sometimes, nothing seems to be going on, and you need to stop and be aware. Be aware, and maybe beware. Self-awareness is a quality which can help you stay in the moment. This may be a moment when you see an opportunity that God put in front of you. Someone may need a smile or a pat on the back. Without self- awareness, you'll miss most of those moments. Be mindful. Self-awareness and mindfulness go together. I believe God wants us to be aware of ourselves and always mindful of the needs of others. God may need to give someone a hug, and you're just the one to give it.

JULY 21, 2018
LADY SNAKE KILLER

Of Mythological snakes, snake charmers, and snake killers. Joseph Campbell, a great mind, and an American authority on mythology was a significant source for learning the truths of ancient legends and mythology. My takeaway from studying Campbell, was the reality of the myth, which often seemed paradoxical, but was always a lesson of truth. Included in his teachings are some stories of mythological herpetology.

My first example comes from Egyptian mythology. This is the story of Apep, a giant serpent, known as the Lord of Chaos. He was the enemy of Ra, the Egyptian Sun God. A great battle took place and Ra whipped up on Apep, thus defeating Chaos, and insuring an orderly existence for the Eighth Dynasty, some 5,000 years ago.

The first real truth for me was the Biblical Creation of Adam and Eve. Unfortunately, there was a Devilish Serpent in the Garden of Eden, and tempted Eve to eat the forbidden fruit, resulting in Humanity's fall from Grace, and the account was later polished up by Milton's, "Paradise Lost."

In Greek mythology, there was a God of Healing,

named Asclepius (make up your own pronunciation), and he carried a long Rod, wrapped by a serpent. Thus, today, we see this symbol on hospitals, clinics, and sometimes on a doctor's lapel.

Another take on the serpent, are the snake charmers. India used to have a lot of snake charmers, and would thrill tourists, playing flutes, and coaxing a poisonous snake to rise up out of a basket. Fortunately the practice has been in decline since 1972, when India passed a law against snake charming. The well-known Hollywood snake charmer is the once very attractive Debra Paget. She had a supporting role in, "Ten Commandments" but was after Joshua, not Moses. She got her snake charming reputation appearing as a sexy dancer in a German film. She was able to make the snake do anything she wanted with her daring moves. On close examination, the serpent was a prop.

After a few bouts with snakes as a young camper in Hunt, Texas, I lost my courage with snakes. Today, I'm not only afraid of snakes, but the image of them turns my stomach. I have killed a few snakes in my life, but nothing to write about. Most of us have seen or read about the mongoose, and its great snake killing ability. But the greatest snake killer for my money is my bride of over 30 years. This week, there was a rather large viper moseying around outside on our deck. We decided there wasn't a good opportunity to kill it, and since I was late to a downtown meeting, I told her it would just wander back to its home, down by the river. Fifteen minutes after I left home, she called me, and I listened to the greatest snake killer of all time. She decided Mr. Snake didn't need to go home, and since she has a concealed carry license, she loaded her .38 special with rat shot and pumped five shots into the large multicolored beast. Needless to say, don't mess with Ms. Powell.

APRIL 14, 2018
MAYBE NEXT WEEK

I just posted my Saturday evening post. Don't know what happened, but when I punched, "POST," I lost my internet, and being the technophobe I am, I lost my post. It seems as though I lose a lot of things these days. It's past my bedtime, so I'm chalking this one off.

MARCH 9, 2019

WILLIE, THE DUKE, AND DR. VICTOR DAVIS HANSON

Who would you choose? Remember the fantasy question asked of Miss America hopefuls? It goes something like this; "If you could spend an evening at dinner with any three people, who would you choose?" If the candidate asked, "Alive or Dead?" Loser!! No, the comely lass had to quickly come up with three persons, and have good reasons for each of them. Well, who would you pick?

My first pick would be Jesus Christ, but then, such a choice would probably be considered a violation of the First Amendment. So, to reply with a thoughtful, intelligent answer I would select a combination of personal heroes. Each hero should be well known, learned, entertaining, and be blessed with significant wisdom.

Here's my picks, John Wayne, Willie Nelson, and Victor Davis Hanson. All three are white men. All three are American patriots, and all would express themselves from both liberal and conservative viewpoints. I thought about including a woman, but these three guys would have been too honed in on being a gentleman. I, the person there to glean knowledge and wisdom, would have been playing second fiddle, thus somewhat ignored. Although all old white men have been tabbed racist, I could just as easily chosen Clarence Thomas, Morgan Freeman, and Bill Russell, all American patriots with liberal and conservative viewpoints.

So, with no more excuses, here are good reasons for my selections. First, John Wayne is a no-brainer. Maureen O'Hara once testified to Congress, "John Wayne is not just an actor, and a very fine actor, John Wayne is the United States of America." She wanted a medal struck for him, and it would simply say, "John Wayne, American." One of his great lines, as Jake Cutter in Comancheros, "Words are what men live by...words they say and mean." I dream of sitting at the table with him as our waiter takes his order, "Bring me a big thick steak, some grilled onions, a baked potato with a lotta butter, and no salad." Robert Mitchum, spoke of him, "His living testimony to his spoken beliefs contribute respect to that image...As a man, he has achieved his place with dignity."

Willie Nelson is a bit more difficult to define as heroic. If you consider 85 years of hard living, his mistakes, his successes, his outlook on life, his friends, and achievements, one must consider this fellow Texan as a bigger than life, true American Hero." Read his book, "The Tao of Willie: A guide to the happiness in your heart." My first clue to his philosophic wisdom, is the quote, "Fortunately we are not in control." Willie had enough control to write over two thousand songs, sell millions of records, give thousands of concerts, and act in a few movies. You can learn a bunch, spending an afternoon reading the, "Tao of Willie." The book is a compendium on how to live life. How can you tell it any better; "To be a servant of God, we must love unselfishly, and when everyone does this we will have heaven right here on earth." Now there's some truth folks!

Now, to my newest hero, Victor Davis Hanson. He is the Martin and Illie Anderson Senior Fellow in classics and military history at the Hoover Institution, Stanford University. He has written over twenty books, and submits economic, historical, and political articles on a weekly basis. His most recent work is titled, "The Case for Trump," Dr. Hanson could easily be improperly defined as an intellectual elite, of the, "Left Coast." Having read some of his writings, learned of his family history, and listened to him speak, I consider him a genius, and a true, American patriot. His family settled on a small farm in the California San Joaquin Valley, and Dr. Hanson lives in the home his great-great-great grandfather built in 1870. His family continues to operate the farm today. Coming from an American pioneer family, growing up on a small farm, I know he would win the respect of John Wayne and Willie Nelson.

Sharing an evening with these three American Patriots, is indeed an imaginary, storybook, mountain top event only to be dreamed. Maybe we will meet on the other side. In Willie's book, he writes how he has learned to keep his mouth shut. Being such a prolific songwriter, guitar picking singer, I think for him to learn when to shut up as real experiential wisdom. I have taken this wisdom, and with a bit of success, I am trying to learn to shut up. Definitely a work in progress, I pray my effort will ultimately gain dividends.

> "My heroes have always been cowboys,
> And they still are it seems.
> Sadly in search of, and one step in back of,
> Themselves, and their slow-movin dreams."
> Lyrics by Sandra Vaughn, sung by Willie and me.

FEBRUARY 2, 2019
TOBACCO JUICE

To spit or not to spit; that is the dilemma.

If you are alone in the forest, it's O.K. Not alone, and in populated areas; the dilemma arises. It is a natural human reaction and pleasing experience to rid one's mouth of, well, you know what I mean. To swallow, the reverse of spitting, may not be the healthier alternative. So, ever since humans roamed the world, and the sidewalks, spitting has been a necessary behavior, even when, at times the practice has not been considered acceptable.

Over time, spitting has primarily been carried out by the male sex. China is the exception. Chinese grannies have a special ritual of spitting. It usually occurs during mealtime. It begins as a guttural, hawking sound deep in the throat, until it reaches the front of the mouth and is forced out onto the floor. I have never witnessed such a performance, and I hope I never will, but when it comes to the art of expectoration, the Chinese rule the world. You may ask how did I come by such information, and as with most of my recently learned knowledge I discovered the practice while surfing the big internet wave in search of a topic for my post.

In my early years, spitting was part of early childhood development. Spitting, or maybe spitting up, was an infant reaction to getting more milk than was necessary. Once we learned how not to eat or drink more than the appropriate serving, spitting is reduced, and our childhood development reaches a more advanced state. Growing up in Texas, I learned to spit watermelon seeds quite a far piece. Usually in my grandmother's back yard we would have grand watermelon seed spitting contests. Everyone would win a prize; another piece of watermelon.

During the 19th century, America grew up. In the new fancy urban areas, local ordinances were passed to limit spitting for the good of the country. Railroad cars were required to place a brass spittoon at each end of a passenger car, and travelers were required to use the vessels for all expectoration, or be fined. I was unable to uncover the size of the fine, but my inkling is, it was not substantial, and you could probable just spit in the isle if the conductor wasn't watching. Where sidewalks were built, it was usually OK to spit in the street. During these years, the art of spitting tobacco juice came into play.

Tobacco juice has been the expectorant with the greatest popularity. This practice continues to this day. Some of my best friends have spit cups in their pick-up trucks, and even in their golf carts. I have never learned the art of spitting tobacco juice. I gave it the old college try many years ago, but it made me sick as hell, and I had to give it up. There have probably been scholarly research studies to determine the unhealthiness of chewing smokeless tobacco; however, I chose to use Marlboros as my tobacco of choice. As we all know, those things will kill us, so at the young age of 38, I gave up smoking, a discontinued enjoyable habit, which did not include spitting, and one of the healthiest decisions of my life.

I spent a bit of time trying to run down how the term, "Spitten Image," got its origin. There is considerable disagreement among a number of linguists how the term came to be. So much so, frustration took hold, and I just let it go. Safe it to say, if your Daddy is a good looking dude, and someone says, "You're the spitten image of your old man," take it as a compliment.

There have been some great western movies which included some spectacular spitting. Sometimes a brass spittoon was in the scene, and other times the spittee was a Yankee carpetbagger. Clint Eastwood played the Outlaw Josey Wales, and he frequently spit tobacco juice wherever he wanted. Sometimes it was an insult, and sometimes it just landed on cactus. I don't know if Clint had a double for the spitting scenes, but if not, Mr. Eastwood would be eligible for all current spitting contests.

So, to spit or not to spit. I have never spit on another person. Lately, I have contemplated such a decision. There are a number of politicians who might be humbled if they felt a little unwelcome spit. But like the guy said, "You're going to spit on a U.S. Senator?" I would have to say, "Gosh, I know I wanna."

DECEMBER 29, 2018

UNDERWEAR FOR THE NEW YEAR

You can stick a fork in the, "Year of the Dog." It's done. Get ready to welcome the, "Year of the Pig." Just a bit of Oriental Zodiac to get you ready for the great big ball to drop in Times Square.

The ball has a bit of history. The first one dropped in 1907, and it weighed in at 500 pounds. This New Year's Eve, the giant, spherical stopwatch is 12 feet in diameter, with 2,688 Waterford Crystal triangles; It tips the scales at 11,875 pounds, lit up with 32,256 LED lights, and promises to amaze everyone with a kaleidoscopic effect. The weather forecast for Midtown Manhattan is cold and rainy, and umbrellas are not permitted. I can think of over a hundred things, no, that would be a thousand things I would rather do than celebrate the New Year's Eve of the Pig, in person, on an island worth $24 of beads, or was it some wampum worth 24 beads?

Oh well, the big ball drop is an American tradition, and I will try and keep my eyes open, Monday night, until 11:00

central standard, South Texas, flyover country time. We won't be going out tonight. My back will go out before I do.

I think each new year should be an occasion to get rid of some of the old and begin looking around for stuff that will be old in 12 months. But, some of our friends around the world have some weird traditions to welcome in Bonne Annee. In Denmark, people who like you will break plates on your front porch. I'm not kidding. Look it up! In Johannesburg, South Africa, people throw out old furniture. If you're driving around next week, you might find some real bargains on some used furniture.

In some of the countries south of us, underwear has special meanings on New Year. In Columbia, wearing yellow underwear will bring you happiness and good fortune. I don't think that's going to go over very well, across the border in Venezuela. In Brazil, wearing pink will help your love life. Pink goes well in Bolivia also, but you need to wear it backwards. Whatever one does in the South American countries, don't wear black undies on New Year's Eve. Doing so, is a sign of evil, and will bring bad luck.

I've always been interested in the Oriental year of the snake, and have ascribed it a personal meaning of negativity. It got my attention when I looked up some snake years in the past. 1929 the stock market crashed, 1941 the Japanese attacked Pearl Harbor, 2001 was 9-11. The good news is the year of the snake won't return until 2025, so we have some time to prepare.

Although most New Year's resolutions won't be kept, I think it's good to set some goals and make some plans. Don't worry, you can always modify your goals, and change your plans. It's good to be flexible and even Marines adapt. So, I sincerely wish everyone a Happy and Prosperous 2019!

Printed in the United States
By Bookmasters